Praise for Walking in Beauty

"*Walking in Beauty* invites readers to open our eyes—and hearts —to the abundance of beauty in the world. The offerings of daily practices and rituals, along with magical recipes and Phoenix's own insights on this work, serve as a buffer to our rough edges and lead us down a glorious road back to beauty. *Walking in Beauty* is the perfect antidote to these troubling times. Such a treasure!"

—Dani Burlison, editor of *All of Me: Stories of Love, Anger, and the Female Body*

"Thoughtful … necessary … delightful … and timely. *Walking in Beauty* by Phoenix LeFae is a breath of fresh, beautiful air amidst a culture and era steeped in trauma and crisis. Through a gentle re-conditioning of thought, the author subtly trains us to refocus our vision and remember the beauty all around us, catching us by the collar and hauling us back in the nick of time, just before we dive off the cliff into despair."

—Katrina Rasbold, author of *The Sacred Art of Brujería: A Path of Healing & Magic*

"Phoenix LeFae has done more than simply write a book. She has gifted us with a jewel. *Walking in Beauty* is gentle and lovely, but also power-filled and empowering. It leads with the heart into our collective soul."

—Courtney Weber, author of *The Morrigan: Celtic Goddess of Magick and Might*

D1563490

WALKING
in
BEAUTY

About the Author

Phoenix LeFae is equal parts blue-eyed wanderer and passionate devotee to several deities. She is a restless seeker of knowledge, always yearning to learn more, dig deeper, and dive into mystery. Phoenix encourages the whims of her divine muses to push her forward, which manifests in writing, ritual, teaching, and devotion. Her journey on the path of Witchcraft started in 1994 when her athame was a wooden-handled butter knife stolen from her mom's kitchen. Her love of magick and mystery lead her down many paths, lineages, and traditions. She is an initiate in the Reclaiming Tradition of Witchcraft, the Avalon Druid Order, and Gardnerian Wicca. She has had the pleasure of teaching and leading ritual across the United States, Canada, and Australia. She is a hoodoo practitioner, professional Witch, published author, and the owner of the esoteric Goddess shop Milk & Honey in Sebastopol, California (www.Milk-and-Honey .com).

PHOENIX LeFAE

WALKING
in
BEAUTY

USING *the* MAGICK *of*
the PENTACLE *to*
BRING HARMONY
to YOUR LIFE

Llewellyn Publications
Woodbury, Minnesota

FIRST EDITION
First Printing, 2020

Cover design by Shira Atakpu
Editing by Hanna Grimson
Interior illustrations by the Llewellyn Art Department

Llewellyn Publications is a registered trademark of Llewellyn Worldwide Ltd.

Library of Congress Cataloging-in-Publication Data
Names: LeFae, Phoenix, author.
Title: Walking in beauty : using the magick of the pentacle to bring
    harmony to your life / [Phoenix LeFae].
Description: First edition. | Woodbury, Minnesota : Llewellyn Publications, 2020.
    | Includes bibliographical references. | Summary: "Using the pentacle and its five
    points as a magickal framework, this book presents techniques and exercises to
    run the energy of the Beauty Pentacle through the body to clear blocks as well
    as to manifest joy, discover inner and outer beauty, recognize blessings, and bring
    balance to the reader's life. Through exercises, rituals, and beauty acts, Phoenix
    LeFae presents an approach based on the five points of the Beauty Pentacle-beauty,
    devotion, desire, creativity, and expression"— Provided by publisher.
Identifiers: LCCN 2020011062 (print) | LCCN 2020011063 (ebook) | ISBN
    9780738762555 (paperback) | ISBN 9780738764948 (ebook)
Subjects: LCSH: Witches. | Feminine beauty (Aesthetics)—Miscellanea. |
    Pentacles. | Magic.
Classification: LCC BF1571.5.W66 L46 2020 (print) | LCC BF1571.5.W66
    (ebook) | DDC 133.4/3—dc23
LC record available at https://lccn.loc.gov/2020011062
LC ebook record available at https://lccn.loc.gov/2020011063

Llewellyn Worldwide Ltd. does not participate in, endorse, or have any authority or respon-sibility concerning private business transactions between our authors and the public.
    All mail addressed to the author is forwarded but the publisher cannot, unless specifically instructed by the author, give out an address or phone number.
    Any internet references contained in this work are current at publication time, but the publisher cannot guarantee that a specific location will continue to be maintained. Please refer to the publisher's website for links to authors' websites and other sources.

Llewellyn Publications
A Division of Llewellyn Worldwide Ltd.
2143 Wooddale Drive
Woodbury, MN 55125-2989
www.llewellyn.com

Printed in the United States of America

Other Books by Phoenix LeFae

Hoodoo Shrines and Altars

Cash Box Conjure

What Is Remembered Lives

Forthcoming Books by Phoenix LeFae

Life Ritualized

This book is dedicated to the planet:
the most beautiful creature I have ever seen.

Contents

Disclaimer   xiii

Introduction: Beginnings   1

Part One: An Introduction to the Pentacle

Chapter 1: The World Needs Beauty   11

Chapter 2: Basics: Ritual and Deities   19

Chapter 3: Working with Pentacles   37

Chapter 4: Working with the Beauty Pentacle   49

Part Two: The Points

Chapter 5: Beauty   71

Chapter 6: Devotion   101

Chapter 7: Creativity   129

Chapter 8: Desire   157

Chapter 9: Expression   185

Part Three: Expanding and Going Beyond

Chapter 10: Advanced Workings   217

Chapter 11: Guerrilla Acts of Beauty   243

Chapter 12: Staying Connected to Beauty   253

Acknowledgments 257

Recommended Reading   259

Bibliography   261

Disclaimer

This book is not a replacement for physical or mental health care. Don't follow any of the directions or rituals in this book if they have the potential to harm you physically or mentally. If you are currently under medical supervision, maintain that contact while reading this book. Don't push yourself or try anything that would bring you harm. If at any time you are worried about harming yourself, please call the National Suicide Prevention Hotline for help: 800-273-8255.

Introduction
Beginnings

Imagine strolling through a lush, dense forest. With each step you can hear the crunch of leaves beneath your feet. The sunlight streams through the canopy, creating patterns of shadow across the forest floor. You breathe in and smell the damp, sweet odor of fresh growth mixed with the decomposition of the loam under your feet. The chatter of birds is carried on the wind. When the sound hits your ears, you feel a tightness in your chest begin to soften and a smile crosses your lips. Walking through the forest is a simple pleasure, but it is one filled with beauty.

Sometime around 2010 I co-taught a weeklong intensive at California Witchcamp. My co-teacher and I offered a five-day workshop called Walking in Beauty. It was dubbed by the campers as the "bardic path" because the plan was to incorporate poetry and writing with magick and Witchcraft. The goal of this class was to tap into our creative selves and express them in a myriad of artistic ways. We had a clear vision and a direction, but over the week the magick that we were doing evolved into so much more—way more than I ever expected.

The flow of our class became less and less about poetry or tapping into our magickal bardic powers and more about finding beauty. But the words "finding beauty" aren't quite the right words for what happened either. Our group of twenty Witches and edge walkers opened up to *remembering* beauty and seeing beauty in all of the things that are happening around us all of the time. Our path became a place where we could share the beauty that we were discovering with other people. We found that the more we opened our eyes to the beauty of the world, the more we could see it. Concurrently, by sharing these discoveries with other people not taking our workshop, we were able to help open *their* eyes to this beauty too. We discovered that awakening to beauty grows and expands on itself exponentially. One of the tools we used to do this work was the Beauty Pentacle.

Shortly after the initial *Walking in Beauty* workshop, I had an experience with an ancestor. She told me it was time to bring the tool of the Beauty Pentacle into the world. She said that humanity needs to be reminded of how much beauty there is. She told me that it is too easy to be focused on what is wrong, broken, and terrible. It is too easy to lose the threads of beauty. It is part of the modern illness of disconnection, and beauty is the cure.

And I don't say this from a place of fluffy, surface, easy magick. Connecting to beauty is hard. It is a challenge. This process and practice has revolutionized who I am as a Witch.

The word *awesome* has been watered down in our modern lexicon. Awesome doesn't hold the weight and gravitas that it once did. The actual definition of the word awesome is "something that inspires awe." The definition of awe is "a feeling of reverential respect mixed with fear or wonder." Can you think of a time when you have been struck with reverential fear or wonder?

Seriously, think about a time that you felt true awe. Go on, I'll wait. … Did you feel that? The awe, reverence, that *wonder* is the power of the Beauty Pentacle. It is more than a power; it is a living force.

It is so easy to see the devastation, the horror, the ugliness of the world, but the truth is that the world is *awesome*. Even within the challenges and terrors there are moments of beauty so magnificent that it stops the breath and quiets the mind. It is in the experience of magnificence that the Beauty Pentacle was born. And using the Beauty Pentacle can awaken that feeling in us every day. It serves as a reminder to what is always available.

The Beauty Pentacle is both a meditation tool and a key to greater awareness. At its core the Beauty Pentacle is an energy force, and that force can be run through our physical bodies. Moving this energy allows it to serve us as a tool and awaken our senses to the beauty and power of the world around us. Running the energy of the Beauty Pentacle through the pentacle of our living human body, we awaken our creative, dynamic selves. The tool that is the Beauty Pentacle lays over our physical bodies, which are also pentacles. Our head and five limbs create a star *(pentagram),* and the energy that flows between those five points creates a circle around the star *(pentacle)*. We will explore this more as you read on. The energy of the Beauty Pentacle feeds us and opens us up with more awareness to the beautiful web of life.

Incorporating the Beauty Pentacle into your everyday life is so much more than smelling the roses and turning a blind eye to difficulties. It's easy to connect the word *beauty* with something superficial, like ignoring the troubles of the world or skipping through fields of grain. The Beauty Pentacle is not about turning away from the troubles of the world, but rather, it is a turning towards what is magickal in the world. We can hold both; in fact we must hold both. The Beauty Pentacle is a calling to connect to the beautiful because it is easy to forget that it is there.

The earth is a miracle. Humans are miracles. Every single thing we do, see, smell, taste, and experience is a miracle. All of it. The good, the bad, the challenging, the easy, the boring; all of it, miracles.

Just the fact that millions of years ago a creature climbed out of the muck and over time evolved into a woman sitting on her couch typing out language on an electronic device that connects her to information all over the world is pretty spectacular. It's easy to forget that.

Although the focus of this tool isn't to come to terms with societal expectations of what beauty means, your feelings around this are likely to come up as you learn to use this device. The more you connect to the magick that is beauty, the more beautiful you will feel. It is our birthright, beauty. The Beauty Pentacle reconnects us to the greater world and our role in it.

We are not *apart* from that world. In fact, we are a part *of* it. Opening our eyes to the beauty in the leaves, the mountains, the flowers, the birds, the ocean, reminds us that we are also the leaves, the mountains, the flowers, the birds, and the ocean. We are connected. All of us and everything are connected.

It is easy to forget that what happens on the other side of the planet impacts my place on the globe. It is easy to get caught up in the day-to-day needs of life. It is easy to get sucked into fighting on social media or the drama of television news. But there is so much more going on in the world.

The Beauty Pentacle asks you to remember.

Throughout this book you will have opportunities to do some of your own exploration of the Beauty Pentacle. There will be exercises, journaling prompts, and guerrilla acts of beauty for you to take out into the world. You can work through this book one section at a time, letting the energy of the Beauty Pentacle flow through you in a more linear order. Or you can allow yourself to be drawn to different pages, prompts, and offerings randomly in order to let the beauty flow with your intuition. No matter how you decide to work through this book, I would encourage you to start with the Working with Pentacles section. This will give you a solid foundation of how this tool works and how to run it through your body.

In each section there will be more than one *Check-In*. These are writing prompts where you will have the opportunity to explore your feelings on a specific topic. But don't feel that a journaling prompt must be writing an essay. Feel free to explore the *Check-Ins* as an art piece, a dance, a walk through your neighborhood. Let each *Check-In* move through you and express it in the way that feels right.

Throughout the book there will be lots of opportunities to practice the working of the pentacle points. Exercises titled *Discovering Beauty, Devotion, Creativity, Desire,* or *Expression* will provide opportunities for you to play with the pentacle points and work with the individual power of each of them more deeply. These exercises will show you where you may have blocks or obstacles you need to work on.

You will have an opportunity for more advanced work in *Expanding and Going Beyond* and many different ways to run the energy of the Beauty Pentacle through your body and work with the energy of the pentacle points. These sections can help you to clear blocks or obstacles that may be keeping you from living a fully-engaged and beautiful life.

There is also a chapter full of prompts for *Guerrilla Acts of Beauty*. These are challenges and opportunities for you to take the Beauty Pentacle out into the world. These challenges are best done in stealth mode so that no one knows who did the beautiful act. Most of the time you won't get to see the experience you've created for another person to receive. The point is not to take credit for it, but to pass it on. The best guerrilla acts of beauty are the ones that you create, mold, paint, scheme, write, and conspire to create yourself. The guerrilla acts offered in this book are just a jumping-off point. Let your imagination go with this concept. Pass on the beauty as much and as often as you can.

The most important part of this book is to remember beauty.

FEAR

It is impossible to focus on all of the beauty in the world without having fears creep in. Being able to love means being willing to lose the thing we love. Feeling pain or fear helps us to remember beauty. It is a precarious, and precious, balance. We can't feel the highs without also feeling the lows. In fact, it is the lows that help us to really taste the sweetness of the highs.

With all of the despair that is so prevalent in the world, it can feel disrespectful to celebrate the beauty. For many of us there may also be an underlying worry that connecting to beauty is frivolous or trivial. Celebrating beauty through our fears is a revolutionary act.

Fear should not be avoided but embraced. Fear can work as a bridge that reconnects us to beauty. Remember, we are only guaranteed this one life. We can't truly know what happens after death. It is important that we live for today and not for some uncertain afterlife that may never materialize. We know for certain that the cycle of life on this planet is real. Plants grow, fed by the nutrients in the earth. Animals eat those plants, and then we eat the plants and animals. One day we will die, and our bodies will return to the ground to create nutrients for the plants. This cycle is all we truly know for sure.

This moment—this moment right now—is all that we are guaranteed. This moment is the only truth there is. It is our only guarantee. It is a disservice to ourselves and this life to not soak up every beautiful moment of it.

Walking in Beauty asks us to remember that the world isn't just something we take from. The planet is not an unending resource that humans can just deplete. The earth is us. Every beautiful piece of it is us. This isn't just New Age woo, it is science. The universe was created from star dust and explosion. Every piece of the planet is made up of those same origins. We are of that stuff too.

DISCOVERING BEAUTY
Beauty Journal

Your first official home adventure for this working is to get yourself a journal to use just for exploring the Beauty Pentacle. The best journal is one that can handle different forms of media. You may want to draw, write, paint, glue in images, press flowers, or a myriad of other expressions. Pick a journal that can handle all of these art mediums. You should also find this journal beautiful. You should want to hold it in your hands, add to it, be with it, and create.

✦ ✦ ✦ CHECK-IN ✦ ✦ ✦

What comes up for you when you hear the word *beauty*? How do you feel about this word from an internal perspective? How do you feel about this word from an external perspective? How do you feel that beauty impacts your life? Give yourself some time to write your answers to these questions.

Part One

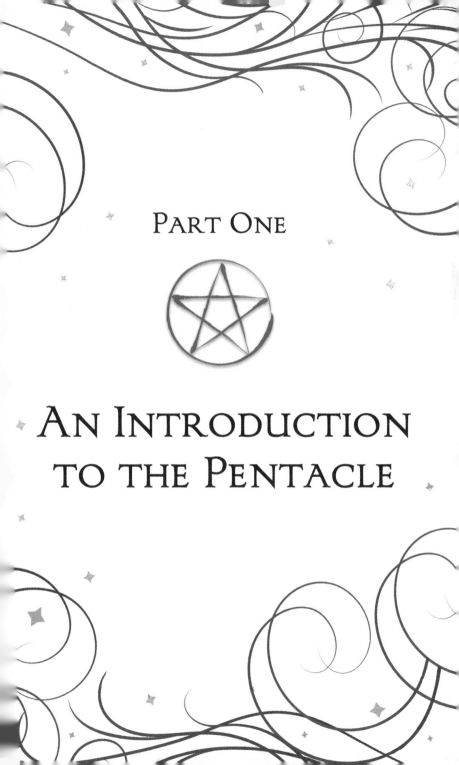

An Introduction to the Pentacle

CHAPTER 1
THE WORLD NEEDS BEAUTY

All it takes is five minutes on social media, two minutes watching a news channel, or a paragraph-worth of online news to feel bombarded with all of the terrible things going on in the world. You don't have to look very hard to get it. Things are rough.

I've got some good news for you. It is even *easier* to find beauty in the world. All it takes is looking out of a window. It might not pop up immediately, but wait, take a breath, there is magick in the patience. Keep watching out your window and something beautiful will happen. I guarantee it. There is an un-limited amount of beauty just waiting for you to see it. It might be a bird flying by, a cloud formation, the scent of cooking food from a neighbor's house, the sound of children playing, or the stars twinkling in the sky; beauty is there.

Seeing the beauty is one thing, but there is more to this work than sitting back and passively watching. What makes the Beauty Pentacle a powerful tool is that it needs to be shared. When you see something that strikes you with awe and wonder, show that to someone else. When you witness an act of kindness, tell that story. When you are moved by an interaction with another being, share that interaction. Pay it forward. The gift must move.

Beauty is a power that resides within each one of us. It is a power that is uniquely human. It is also a tool that is uniquely you. The Beauty Pentacle is a spiritual tool that helps us to harness the power of beauty and direct it for healing ourselves and the world around us. Once you learn how to harness that energy it becomes a tool that you can move through your body. It becomes a tool of vision, allowing you to see truth in the world. And it becomes a technique that can aid in meditation and grounding.

This book is an invitation to step into the flow of beauty in your life. Reading this book is an exclamation of, "Yes! I will honor the beauty of the world, and I will share that with others." The Beauty Pentacle is a tool and technique to help you shift the focus of your eyes and awaken a powerful energy within you. Are you ready to step into the flow?

The Pentacle and The Body

Take a moment to lie down right now. Extend your arms and spread your legs. Stretch out your neck as long as you can and feel the edges of your body. Your body is a living pentagram, a five-pointed star. You already live and breathe sacred geometric energy just by having a physical form. The Beauty Pentacle is made up of five points that overlay your physical body. In the following pages, each point of the pentacle will have its own chapter, giving you the opportunity to dive deeply into that specific point and explore how it fits in your own life.

There are layers to this type of work. There will be your external process with the Beauty Pentacle and your internal process.

There will be how you run this energy through your body and how it feels physically. This tool will also change the way you look at the world and how you interact with others. All of these pieces will provide insight on where you may have obstacles, blockages, or places where you need to give some clarity and focus.

The Points

The points of the pentacle are: *beauty, devotion, creativity, desire,* and *expression.*

The first point, *beauty,* is an obvious one, but it is also complex. The energy center of beauty is the overarching point of this book. This "point" is actually more of a sphere of power that resides in the top of your head. It is the connection to your god-self and your third eye. The beauty point is how we connect to the power of this tool. It is from this place that the energy flows to all the other points. This is connected to the beauty in the world, the beauty in your heart, the beauty of your body; all of these things and more are part of the point of beauty.

The second point in the pentacle is *devotion.* This is your relationship to the greater world around you, both the tangible and intangible parts of it. Devotion also asks us how we spend our energy and what we are willing to put ourselves on the line for. What are you devoted to? Who are you devoted to? How and why are you devoted to yourself? How does that devotion inform how you look at the world? How is that beautiful?

The third point of the pentacle is *creativity,* which is your personal outpouring of beauty. Creativity asks you to take the beauty that you have seen and do something with it. How does the beauty of the world connect to your creative self? How does your internal beauty spark creativity in your life? Do you feel like a creative person? How do creativity and beauty meet in you? Creativity is the place where you can put the beauty you've held.

The fourth point is *desire*, and this is the spark that calls you to action. When the awe of beauty becomes so full and potent, when you've taken in so much beauty that you feel like you just can't hold it all in, that is the power of desire. It is the pinnacle of input before output is necessary. Desire is the fuel of the pentacle. What do you desire? How does that desire make you feel?

The fifth and final point is *expression*, which is the release of that desire. Expression gives you a place to share the beauty that you have been holding. It is a sharing of your beauty with the world. Expression allows for what you've been holding to be released and become bigger than yourself. How do you express yourself? Are you honest with your expression?

Before we move on to some of the more subtle functions of this work, I want to address the difference between the title of the whole pentacle and the specific beauty point, both called by the same name. The Beauty Pentacle is named for the first energy point. The flow of power is rooted in beauty; as it moves through the pentacle it begins at the top of your head, as if an invoking pentacle is being drawn on you. The energy flow starts with beauty and ends with beauty. Therefore, the name of this tool is the Beauty Pentacle. The beauty point—or energy center—is the micro, while the overarching energy of the pentacle is the macro.

BRIGHT SHADOW

There is a side effect of the Beauty Pentacle. It is a phenomenon that I was taught by Copper Persephone, one of my mentors, in 2009 called the *bright shadow*. Working on your bright shadow is not the purpose of this tool, but it is bound to happen because the energy of the bright shadow is closely related to the energy of the Beauty Pentacle.

We Witches and Pagans often talk about exploring our hidden shadows. We talk about our shadows as if they are bad, negative, harmful parts of ourselves (and they could be). We participate in rituals to help us heal our shadows. We meditate on raising our shadows up into our conscious awareness. We take workshops and classes to help us find balance with our hidden shadow selves. By having awareness of our shadows, we become stronger.

The hidden shadows of our spiritual psyche are often connected to wounds, hurts, triggers, and challenges that we don't quite know how to deal with. They may be issues buried in our subconscious. Facing those shadows, healing what can be healed, and understanding the parts that need more time to heal is powerful human work—work that should lead us to a greater sense of wholeness.

By incorporating the Beauty Pentacle into your life, it is likely that you will be faced with pieces of your hidden shadow that need healing. And conversely, you are just as likely to find yourself facing parts of your bright shadow that need acknowledging.

The bright shadow is made up of the pieces of yourself that are big, talented, skilled, amazing, and wonderful. We all have these parts and pieces and some of us really know it. Some of us know how to own our bright selves. There are folks who can stand tall and accept the acclaim when it comes their way. However, this isn't true for everyone. Sometimes accepting how powerful we are is difficult. Sometimes we might not think we deserve to shine. We may have wounds, hurts, or triggers that are connected to how strong we really are. Accepting the bright shadows, revealing them, letting them shine, and welcoming them into our consciousness can be just as difficult as facing the hidden shadows.

Owning your bright shadow isn't about arrogance or thinking you are better than others. In fact, that's hidden shadow sneaking into the action. When you become aware of your bright shadows, you learn to accept your beauty, your strengths, and your skills in a way that is right sized. Beauty reveals the bright shadows and asks you to accept the parts of yourself that are magnificent. Beauty asks for your bright shadows to shine and glow.

In the book *Make Magic of Your Life*, author T. Thorn Coyle asks the reader to think of larger-than-life things that take up just the right amount of space.[1] She lists objects like a mountain, a humpback whale, and the moon as examples of things that take up a lot of space, but it is the right amount of space, and they do it without apology or playing small. She extrapolates this to looking at the larger-than-life humans in your life. What is it about these types of people that is compelling, irritating, frustrating, or admirable? This is the awareness of the bright shadow.

Part of the bright shadow is living your life to the largest capacity you can. This work asks you to stop playing small and step fully into the light and bask in that glory. This is not done with ego or arrogance but owning your beauty in all its forms.

Imagine what your life could be like if you were able to hold your bright shadow as a badge of success. The Beauty Pentacle asks how you can start to live from that place right now. What are the first steps that you need to take to bring that to fruition?

If you are the type of person that hides your light under a bushel, downplays your accomplishments, or deflects celebration of your skills, owning your bright shadow might be a challenge

---

1. Coyle, *Make Magic of Your Life*, 214.

for you. To test your relationship with your bright shadow, the next time you receive a compliment, notice your first reaction. Can you accept the compliment and step into the limelight?

Shadow vs. Bright Shadow

This is not a subject of "darkness" or shadow being negative and "lightness" or bright shadow being good. Hidden shadows are not inherently bad. There is much that hidden shadows can reveal to us. Our shadows exist for important reasons, both hidden and bright. But ignoring them, keeping them hidden, or blaming them for bad behavior does us no good. All personal or spiritual exploration is about coming into a greater state of wholeness. It is not about delineating what is "good" or "bad." Ultimately good and bad make up a false binary. Nothing in this world is clearly this or that. Magick is much more complicated than that, and the human spiritual psyche doubly so.

✦ ✦ ✦ CHECK-IN ✦ ✦ ✦

What is your current relationship with your bright shadow? Are you comfortable and incorporated with your shining parts or is there improvement to be made? How might you start to shine openly and honestly? If you find yourself struggling to see your bright shadow, start by asking your close friends, family, and loved ones what shiny parts they see in you.

Chapter 2
Basics:
Ritual and Deities

This is not an introduction to Witchcraft book, so I'm not going to go into a play by play on how to perform a ritual. However, in the following chapters I make some assumptions on what you might already know. Just in case you don't already know, here are some basic bits of information to help you get through the rituals.

As with anything I teach or write, please make adjustments to any of these exercises and rituals to fit your favorite way to make magick. And if you have lots of experience with ritual and magick, feel free to skip this section.

I split rituals into five basic sections. Each of these areas can be moved and adjusted to fit your needs. This is how I prefer rituals to flow, and a lot of this skeleton comes from the way rituals are laid out in the Reclaiming Tradition of Witchcraft. However, there are lots of other ways to create rituals. Start here and then make them your own.

Tools

Before moving into the parts of ritual, I first want to address the tools that will come up in this book. No tools, except for your body, are required to do the work of the Beauty Pentacle. In many of the rituals, an athame is suggested. This is a sacred ritual knife that is used only for magickal purposes. If you don't have an athame, substitute a wooden wand or the first two fingers of your dominant hand to direct the energy instead of the ritual knife.

Orientation

It's a good idea to know the directions of your space before starting a ritual. In many of the exercises in this book, you will be asked to call the directions or the elements. Knowing where north, south, west, and east are in your home will make it easier for the rituals going forward. It is also helpful to determine the directions when you do rituals outdoors. This is all part of becoming more familiar with your environment.

Ritual Section One: Cleansing & Grounding

In all religious systems there are rules about your level of cleanliness before you enter the temple space. This isn't just about getting the dirt out from under your nails or scrubbing the back of your neck. Yes, part of it is about your physical cleanliness, but it is also about the cleanliness of your spiritual body. When entering a holy place, you want to treat it with respect. As Witches and Pagans, everywhere is our holy place. So, we have a lot to live up to.

One of the foundations of my spiritual practice is cleansing. It is always a good time to do a cleansing. I'm often asked by my spiritual counseling clients if they should cleanse. My response is always, "If you felt the need to ask that question, then the answer is yes." People take a shower every day. People soap up their armpits and shampoo their hair, never putting any thought into how dirty their spirit body might be. It is difficult for the Beauty Pentacle to run clearly and cleanly through your body when your spirit body is not a clear and clean channel. Having a regular spiritual cleansing practice will help the power of the Beauty Pentacle to integrate more easily.

We can't help but pick up gunk in our spirit bodies. It is just part of being human. Maybe you cut someone off on the freeway; you felt bad and waved an apology, but they were pissed nonetheless and sent that barb of negativity right to you. You may have had a fight with your teenager, a jealous co-worker, or someone projecting their bad day onto you. The gunk that collects in our spirit bodies may not be any fault of our own, but taking the time and space to clean it up is necessary.

The simplest way to cleanse is to incorporate it into your current bathing routine. In a coming section of this book, I share some recipes for herbal mixes, including a spiritual cleansing mix. You can use these as part of a regular cleansing practice. Ideally, you want to perform a spiritual cleanse at least once a week. But add a cleansing into your day anytime you feel drained or have had a particularly bad day.

Some ways to cleanse include burning herbs and smudging [2] yourself in their smoke, making a spray to spritz around your aura, making a tisane (herbal tea) to add to your bath, asperging yourself with holy water or salt water, using a rattle around your body, or putting together a salt scrub to use in the shower. Any of these options are effective ways to cleanse your spirit body.

---

2. The word "smudge" is an English word and can refer to the process of burning herbs and using the smoke to cleanse the spiritual body. This is not referring to a Native American practice; however, the practices are very similar.

While you are taking the action for your physical and spirit body, it is important that you also shift your mental and emotional energy too. Breathe and release the mental chatter. Focus on your breathing to calm you down and center your focus. Turn your awareness into your belly, your breathing, and your feet on the ground to calm you. Look at three things around you, take a moment to hear three things happening in the distance, and touch three things with your fingers. Connect with your senses to bring yourself into the present.

As you do the work of the Beauty Pentacle, you may notice old stories coming to the surface. You may find that issues you thought well healed are arising again. One way to help process some of these old hurts is with cleansing.

Grounding is a practice of connecting to the earth below you in order to channel energy more effectively. The earth is an excellent magickal partner. She will take from you what no longer serves and compost it, while at the same time filling you up with clean energy and power. Folks occasionally get "ritual hangover" where they feel wiped out, drained, or a little sick after doing big magick. This is very much like how it feels to be hung over from drinking too much alcohol. One way to avoid this problem is to stay grounded, keeping a thread connected to the earth and draining off excess energy or siphoning in more energy when you are starting to feel overwhelmed or depleted.

There are simple ways to ground:

- Place your feet on the ground, breathe deeply, and release any thoughts or distractions that are keeping you from being fully present. Fill your lungs and cycle the air through your blood and body with focused intention.

- Visualize roots sinking into the earth from your feet and branches moving into the sky from the top of your head. Release anything that doesn't serve the work you are doing. Clear the channels of earth and sky with you between them.
- Place your hands on the center of your body with your eyes closed. Pull in your energy and send that down to the center of the earth. Draw up the power of the molten core of the earth into your body, allowing it to clear out what doesn't serve the magick and bring you into a state of presence.

Ritual Section Two: Sacred Space

After you prepare yourself for the ritual, the next step is to create the ritual space. Again, for Witches and Pagans the world is sacred. We are not looking to make a bubble for our ritual and claim that only the inside is sacred and the rest of the world can go to hell. Rather, we are acknowledging that the world is always sacred, and in this space we strive to honor that.

The creation of sacred space is the part of a ritual where you make a container in which you hold your magick. Sometimes a spell or a ritual needs a little time to cook. You cook it in your sacred space. Most often this is done by "casting a circle" or making an energetic boundary between where you are working and the rest of the world. This container holds your ritual until you are ready to release it.

During this part of the ritual, you may also choose to invite in guides and allies. This is the point where there may be elemental invocations (or evocations). Deities may be called at this time. Ancestors may be invited in. Again, this is not to say that they are not always with us, but rather we are setting aside that specific time and place to honor them and work more intentionally with them.

Ritual Section 3: Tofu (or, the Meat of the Ritual)

This is the part of the ritual where you do the thing. In a spell or ritual you are going through all the steps of creating sacred space in order to *DO* something. That something is the meat or tofu. This can vary greatly depending on your intention, the participants, what you hope to achieve, and how much time you have. This may also be the point where you build up the energy for the ritual: sing a song, dance around the room, or raise energy in some other way.

Ritual Section 4: Good-Byes

The good-byes are the closing down of what you have built up. This is the part of the ritual where you release the energy that has been created throughout your working. You say good-bye and thank you to all of the entities, guides, allies, and elementals you may have invited in, and you open up—or release—the energetic boundary that you created.

Ritual Section 5: Cleaning Up

Sometimes there are remnants of a ritual that need to be cleaned up. And there may be some self-care needed too. Don't take the post-ritual experience for granted.

Self-Care: After ritual or intense personal work, make sure that you drink plenty of water. It may also be important for you to eat and refill your body. Notice what your body needs and take care of it. You may notice feeling tired after an intense experience, and you may need to make space after your ritual for downtime and relaxation. Be cautious of the desire to numb yourself. It is better to go for a walk outside rather than plunge into a Netflix binge.

Natural Items: After a ritual you may have natural items to dispose of. Food or drink can be left outside or poured into a sacred place for offerings. Don't eat the food or drink the drinks that you gave as offerings. If you have flowers or plant remnants from a ritual, you can dry these or compost them.

Altar Pieces: Your altar may be filled with extra items or tokens from a ritual. You may choose to leave these or clear them up. Make sure you treat your items with the reverence they deserve. Don't allow your ritual space to become too cluttered, or conversely, don't ignore it and allow it to become dusty and unused.

DEITIES OF THIS WORK

It is not a requirement of the Beauty Pentacle to work with godds. (I used the spelling godds as a word that is more encompassing of deities of all genders.) However, including deities in your work with the pentacle can be helpful and informative. Deities can help to reveal layers of beauty in the world that we might not see on our own. The godds in this chapter are selected because they have already been integral in the development of the Beauty Pentacle. However, any godd can help you with this work. Consider this a jumping-off point.

CHARGE OF THE GODDESS

The Charge of the Goddess, originally written by Doreen Valiente and then later adapted by Starhawk, is a creed that is used by Witches and Pagans all over the globe. Not only is it beautiful, but in the charge we hear the voice of the Goddess come through. We hear her advice and suggestion on how to best connect with her. The lessons of the Beauty Pentacle are found within the words of the charge.

"Listen to the words of the Great Mother, Who of old was called Artemis, Astarte, Dione, Melusine, Aphrodite, Cerridwen, Diana, Arionrhod, Brigid, and by many other names: Whenever you have need of anything, once a month, and better it be when the moon is full, you shall assemble in some secret place and adore the spirit of Me Who is Queen of all the Wise.

You shall be free from slavery, and as a sign that you be free you shall be naked in your rites. Sing, feast, dance, make music and love, all in My Presence, for Mine is the ecstasy of the spirit and Mine also is joy on earth. For My law is love unto all beings. Mine is the secret that opens the door of youth, and Mine is the cup of wine of life that is the cauldron of Cerridwen, that is the holy grail of immortality.

I give the knowledge of the spirit eternal, and beyond death I give peace and freedom and reunion with those that have gone before. Nor do I demand aught of sacrifice, for behold, I am the Mother of all things and My love is poured out upon the earth.

Hear the words of the Star Goddess, the dust of Whose feet are the hosts of Heaven, whose body encircles the universe: I Who am the beauty of the green earth and the white moon among the stars and the mysteries of the waters, I call upon your soul to arise and come unto me. For I am the soul of nature that gives life to the universe. From Me all things proceed and unto Me they must return. Let My worship be in the heart that rejoices, for behold, all acts of love and pleasure are My rituals.

Let there be beauty and strength, power and compassion, honor and humility, mirth and reverence within you. And you who seek to know Me, know that the seeking and yearning will avail you not, unless you know the Mystery: for if that which you seek, you find not within yourself, you will never find it without. For behold, I have been with you from the beginning, and I am That which is attained at the end of desire."

I keep a copy of the Charge of the Goddess on my beauty altar. I often recite it when doing magickal workings. When I've been to public rituals or workshops where it is used, I recite the words along with the ritualist. It unifies us in our practices and shows us a map of diving into the beauty of the world.

NEPHTHYS

When I first created the Beauty Pentacle, it was from inspiration from the goddess Nephthys. As I mentioned earlier in this book, the Beauty Pentacle was born from a weeklong intensive. That year, the mythological story we were using as our guide for the week was about the goddess Isis, who is the sister of Nephthys. As the week progressed, more and more I found myself hearing the voice of Nephthys while we did our work together. More and more I became aware of this "forgotten" sister. Even now, many years later, I pay homage to Nephthys as the divine inspiration for the Beauty Pentacle.

Origins

In ancient Egyptian mythology, Nut (the sky goddess) and Geb (the earth god) loved each other very much. They were connected in a holy union, holding each other through eternity. Together the two of them started the population of the world. Nut gave birth to four children who went on to rule over all of the realms. It took Nut four days to birth her children, the first being Osiris, the second Isis, the third Set, and the final child, Nephthys.

Isis and Nephthys are seen over and over again as the counterpoint to each other. Where Isis stands as the guardian of the portal of life and birth, Nephthys stands as the guardian of the portal of life and death. Although she was not a ruler of the underworld, she served as guide for the transition into that realm.[3]

Her name translates as "Lady of the House," and she was often seen with the hieroglyph for "house" in the crown she wore. Myths of her official rulership are murky, but she was the main mourner for Osiris, which suggests a position of high status.[4] She did give birth to Anubis, son of Osiris, who serves as psychopomp in Egyptian mythology, leading the souls of the dead to the underworld.

Where Nephthys was "ruler of the house," Isis was "ruler of the throne."[5] Here again we see the two sides of a similar coin. Isis took her place among the wealthy and the ruling class, whereas Nephthys held reign in the homes of common people. We have a lot of information about Isis that has survived over

---

3. Jeremy Naydler, *Temple of the Cosmos* (Rochester: Inner Traditions, 1996), 256.

4. Margaret A. Murray, *The Splendor That Was Egypt* (London: Biddles Ltd, 1984), 102.

5. Murray, *The Splendor That Was Egypt*, 106.

time, but very little about Nephthys. I imagine that these two sisters have a lot in common and hold the power and balance of everything between them. Nephthys serves as the spiritual opposite to her sister. One might say playing second fiddle for all of history.

Nephthys and Beauty: The Bright Shadow

You may be wondering how this goddess connects to working with the Beauty Pentacle. I believe that this goddess is *why* the Beauty Pentacle exists. She is the guardian of the bright shadow. Worship of Isis spread throughout Europe, making it as far as England.[6] But the reach of Nephthys didn't make it as far. If Isis is birth and Nephthys is death, then both of their roles are needed for society. The two are equally important, but the worship of Isis made it around the world while Nepthys lived in the shadow of her sister. Getting stuck in the brilliance of another spirit is part of the work of the bright shadow.

Nephthys had to find her power and value while being second fiddle to her sister. She had to find a way to celebrate her bright shadow when no one else in the world could see it. This is why she is the goddess to call upon when you are having trouble seeing your own gifts. If you have ever been accused of hiding your light under a bushel, Nephthys will understand. She can help you to remember how beautiful you are. She can guide you to see the beauty in the world when you might be under the false impression that there isn't any left. She can show you that there is beauty in things that others might find ugly. Nephthys can show you how to step into your bright shadow and shine.

---

6. Murray, *The Splendor That Was Egypt*, 105.

Because of her relationship with death, Nephthys can help you to find beauty in death, endings, and difficult transitions. Painful experiences are no less beautiful than joyful ones. This doesn't mean that difficult times should be sugarcoated or we should live in denial, but rather, we need to find a way to still see and experience beauty even in the most difficult times. This is true power.

Aphrodite

As my work with the Beauty Pentacle evolved, I started to call upon Aphrodite. She felt like an obvious deity to help me take this work to the next level. Aphrodite has been the goddess called upon in many Beauty Pentacle classes and weekend workshops. She is a gentle guide, but also demanding. Aphrodite smiles a sweet smile, motioning for you to look at yourself in the mirror, and then of course, to look at her. She is a goddess of adoration, and through that power she helped me to deepen the flow of the Beauty Pentacle.

Origins

Aphrodite is the Greek goddess of beauty, desire, sexuality, and love. Even folks who aren't familiar with any goddesses at all have likely heard of Aphrodite. She was born when the Titan Cronus severed the genitals of Uranus and tossed them into the sea. There was a great churning of the salty sea water and out of the foam rose the luscious goddess called Aphrodite. She is born of the sea with no mother, only the waves of the ocean. Her name translates as "sea foam."

So captivating was this goddess that Zeus had her married off as quickly as possible to the blacksmith Hephaestus in an attempt to prevent other deities from fighting over her.[7] This didn't work out as Zeus wanted. Hephaestus did all that he could to make Aphrodite happy, but he was not enough for the goddess of love. The god of war, Ares, often caught her eye and got her attention and affection. Even while married, she followed her own rules and had many dalliances with other godds and mortals alike. She also possessed a magick girdle that allowed the wearer to bring forth feelings of love and lust in others.[8] Aphrodite understands the power of beauty and desire and lets nothing stand in her way of enjoying life to the fullest.

As a goddess of love and beauty, she requires her devotees to prove how much they love her. She has high expectations, and when her devotees don't live up to them, her punishments can be swift and harsh. But there is no other goddess that understands the importance of beauty and how to live a beautiful life.

Aphrodite and Beauty: Self-Love

Aphrodite is an important guide of this work because she can show us how to connect to our own beauty. No one could resist the beauty and power of this goddess, and this went beyond just her physical looks. She carries with her an understanding of what it is to be beautiful. Aphrodite is joyful and glamorous. She celebrates her beauty, she revels in it, and she can show you the way to do the same.

The goddess of beauty is the perfect guide in learning how to honor our personal inherent beauty. Aphrodite holds up a mirror and points out all the perfection that exists within you. Life

---

7. Charlene Spretnak, *Lost Goddesses of Early Greece: A Collection of Pre-Hellenic Myths* (Berkeley: Moon Books, 1978), 55.

8. Thomas Bulfinch, *Bulfinch's Mythology*, (New York: Crown Publishers, 1979), 6.

is beautiful, you are beautiful, the world is beautiful. Aphrodite can help show you the truth of that. Aphrodite demands to be honored and she will tell you that you deserve to be honored too. Don't settle for second best, don't sell yourself short, and don't doubt your own beauty—ever.

Aphrodite is the goddess to call upon when you need to love yourself and appreciate your own beauty: internal and external. She is the goddess to help you break the blocks you may have been holding onto around acknowledging your beautiful self. This goddess stands at each point of the Beauty Pentacle—*beauty, devotion, creativity, desire, expression*—and holds the way open for you to explore. All the while she will remind you, you are beautiful. Accept nothing less.

FREYA

In the early life of the Beauty Pentacle, Freya added her power to its flow. She was able to help shift the pentacle into a tool of power. Freya helped the Beauty Pentacle move from its soft and sweet origin into something hard and fierce. There is no other deity that understands the importance of beauty in our lives more than Freya, because she understands how precious life is. Freya carries a lust for the pure pleasure of being alive, and she can help us connect to our own lust for life, and lust in other things too.

Origins

Freya is a fertility goddess from the Norse pantheon that also rules over love and war. She represents fertility, sexuality, and guards over crops, music, flowers, and Fae beings. She is one of the "old" godds coming from the Vanir, the race of deities that existed before Odin and his tribe of the Aesir invaded.[9] Her father is the god of the sea, Njord, and her twin brother, Freyr, is also a god of fertility and wildness.[10]

Her name literally translates as "Lady."[11] There are many arguments that she was a much larger fixture in the Norse and Germanic worlds than has been retained through the years and small smatterings of writing we have left, but we can't know that for sure. However, the fact that her stories survived the battle between the Aesir and the Vanir would lead me to believe that she was an important fixture to the Norse and Germanic people. Freya served as a bargaining piece of the Vanir in keeping the peace.[12] It is likely the invading peoples of this time were unable to stop the worship of this goddess and incorporated her into their pantheon.

The fragments of myth we have left of Freya tell us of her mysterious missing husband Od that she cried amber tears for, that she had a beautiful amber necklace called Brisingamen, that she had a powerful cloak that turned the wearer into a falcon, and that she was given first choice of the fallen warriors to bring to her realms.[13] Through all of her trials and tribulations she carries a tender warrior's heart.

---

9. Kevin Crossley-Holland, *The Norse Myths* (New York: Random House, 1980), 8.

10. Patricia M. Lafayllve, *Freya, Lady, Vanadis: An Introduction to the Goddess* (Denver: Outskirts Press, 2006), 15.

11. Lafayllve, *Freya, Lady, Vanadis*, 15.

12. Lafayllve, *Freya, Lady, Vanadis*, 16.

13. Lafayllve, *Freya, Lady, Vanadis*, 15.

Freya and Beauty: The Warrior's Heart

Freya is the warrior and lover. She knows when to fight and when to make love. She isn't afraid to celebrate her body. She isn't concerned about what others think. She also understands how important it is to surround yourself with beautiful things and the value of having beauty in your life. Freya is not afraid.

This fierce goddess can open you up to your own fierceness. She reminds us that beauty requires bravery. Being willing to step into beauty, notice it, call to it, and share it with others is an act of bravery. Freya connects the work of the Beauty Pentacle to the warrior's heart. The warrior who isn't worried about the what ifs, but steps forward into the lushness of life and celebrates every song, blossom, kiss, caress, whisper, bite, and memory.

Freya is the goddess to call on when fear is keeping you blocked. Ask for Freya's help when you feel undeserving of beauty in your life. Allow Freya to smash through the cultural expectations of what beauty should be, should look like. None of that is true, real, or valid. Beauty is what beauty does. Freya stands as your champion, calling beauty into your life with a warrior's call to arms.

DIONYSUS

As the tool of the Beauty Pentacle continued to evolve, Dionysus started to share his power with it too. This joyful godd connects to the power of the Beauty Pentacle because he celebrates all of life. He revels in the wild, the wine, the luxury, the music, the sex. His stories are filled with tales where he has to prove himself, uncover deceit, fight for his life, and through it all he continues to find a way to celebrate. He always finds a way to celebrate. Always.

Origins

Dionysus is a Greek deity who is the youngest of the godds and the last to take a seat on Mount Olympus. He was twice born, once from his mortal mother and then again from his god father, which is what made him more than just a demigod.

The most well-known story involving the birth of Dionysus starts with Zeus falling in love with a mortal woman named Semele. Semele insists that Zeus show her his true form in order to prove his love to her. However, the true form of an Olympian is more than a mortal can handle. But she insists and upon revealing his true form, Semele is incinerated. However, Zeus is able to save the baby and gives him to nymphs to take care of. There are also tales that he is the son of Persephone, giving him two mothers.[14]

The tales and myths also described Dionysus as a god who loves deeply and passionately. He loves across genders, understanding that love goes beyond physical form. He travels with a band of wild women, is married to a mortal who became immortal—Ariadne—and travels the world spreading joy and mystery wherever he goes.

Dionysus and Beauty: The Celebration

So often we make spiritual work into work. It *can* be hard, challenging, difficult, or triggering. Dionysus asks us if a different perspective is possible. What if the work of it doesn't have to be work, but rather play? What if there is space for our spiritual pursuits to be fun and celebratory? What if we can honor and celebrate beauty

---

14. Vikki Bramshaw, *Dionysos Exciter to Frenzy* (London: Avalonia 2013), Kindle.

and feel like our cups are filled up and overflowing from enjoying all the world has to offer?

Dionysus can show us the way to celebration. This wild godd can help us to revel in the beautiful things. He can take us out into the world to see the miracles that surround us. He can help us to laugh in glee at the flight of a bird, dance with pure abandon while walking through the trees, and weep with joy at the sight of a cloud formation. The world is filled with wonder, and Dionysus can help us to see it.

When overcome with sadness or depression, call on Dionysus. When you are living on, and through, social media, Dionysus can help lead you back into nature. His mysteries are both vast and subtle. He can help you to see the beauty in the big and the small because it is all beautiful. Call on this godd when you need help remembering how to let your heart sing. Call on this godd when you've forgotten that shedding tears can be not only cathartic, but ecstatic. Call on Dionysus as a guide to step back into your wild self.

DEITIES OF BEAUTY

These four godds have guided me in my work with the Beauty Pentacle, and I feel certain that there will be more that will join the team as it goes on. Each godd that comes into contact with the Beauty Pentacle leaves their individual mark on the power of this tool. If you already have a relationship with a specific deity, call on them when running the Beauty Pentacle through your body and see how their energy may fit with the energy of the Beauty Pentacle.

Chapter 3

Working
with Pentacles

The first written record of using a pentacle in connection to magick comes from the *Key of Solomon* in the 1500s, the original origins of which are unknown. One of the more common translations of this text was written in the late 1800s by Samuel Liddell MacGregor Mathers, F. C. Conybeare, and Aleister Crowley. The book is filled with occult, esoteric, and Kabbalistic magical information and symbols. Through the use of these symbols one could trap spirits, perform spells, and gain power.[15]

A pentacle is a five-pointed star, and on a basic level one could argue that the human body is also a pentacle. This is not a new concept. Da Vinci's Vitruvian Man is a prime example of the human body being imagined as a five-pointed star shape. Sacred geometry and using symbols for spiritual purposes is a magickal practice found across cultures.[16] And the use of the human form

---

15. Aleister Crowley, Samuel Liddell MacGregor Mathers, F.C. Conybeare, *The Three Magical Books of Solomon* (Naples: Albatross, 2018), 109–111.

16. Udo Becker, *The Continuum Encyclopedia of Symbols*, trans. Lance W. Garmer (New York: Continuum, 2000), 5–6.

as a pentacle follows along this same concept. Da Vinci didn't design his man as a magick symbol, more of art and science. But truly what is science if not magick?

The famous Greek philosopher Pythagoras used the symbol of the pentagram for many mathematical and esoteric studies, many of which survive in common use today. He connected this symbol to be one of "Divine Blessing."[17] While, at the same time, in Islamic Mysticism it is a symbol of the five elements and the five senses.[18]

Heinrich Cornelius Agrippa was an occultist and scholar who connected the pentacle to the five elements: earth, air, fire, water, and spirit. Agrippa wrote about the sacred pentacles and their capacity to bind negative energy, allure positive spirits for aid, and give us access to the power of holy names. In his writing, Agrippa shared ways to use a pentacle to control or manipulate spirits.[19] By writing the correct words or prayers in the form of a pentacle, Agrippa believed that certain esoteric powers could be contained or utilized to aid the magician.[20]

In modern Pagan practice, Victor Anderson, the founder of the Feri tradition, turned the human form as a living pentacle into part of their religious practice.[21] Even folks who don't prac-

---

17. Apollonios Sophistes, "The Pythagorean Pentacle" Biblioteca Arcana, last modified January 5, 2000, http://opsopaus.com/OM/BA/PP/index.html.

18. Becker, The Continuum Encyclopedia of Symbols, (New York: Continuum, 2000), 216.

19. Henry Cornelius Agrippa, The Fourth Book of Occult Philosophy: The Companion to Three Books of Occult Philosophy, ed. Donald Tyson, trans. Robert Turner (Woodbury: Llewellyn Publications, 2009), 86–88.

20. Agrippa, The Fourth Book of Occult Philosophy, 167.

21. Jane Meredith and Gede Parma, Magic of the Iron Pentacle: Reclaiming Sex, Pride, Self, Power & Passion (Woodbury: Llewellyn Publications, 2016), 3, 7–9.

tice in the Feri tradition, or in the sister tradition of Reclaiming, have likely heard of the Iron Pentacle. Since the creation of the Iron Pentacle (and the Pearl Pentacle) by Victor Anderson in the 1970s, there have been many other pentacle systems born. Although each of these systems are different and unique, they are all based on the same concept of running energy through the body and using the five points—head, hands, feet—as touchstones for self-development and expression.

All magickal pentacles, of which there are quite a few, are at their most basic a diagnostic tool. Just like chakras, Reiki, or the Cauldron of Poesy, an energetic pentacle can be run through your body, giving you information where you may have imbalances, need healing, or have self-improvement work to do. By allowing the energy of different pentacle systems to move through your body, you can discover where you may not be fully engaged with yourself or with the greater world around you.

The Beauty Pentacle is more than just a series of meditations or journaling prompts. The power of this pentacle will develop the more you use it and share what breakthroughs you have with the world. It begins as a diagnostic tool, or a meditation device, but it grows into something more. It is not something you can just ponder; it is something that you need to experience.

Most pentacles are run through the body as if the Goddess were drawing the pentacle over you. The top of your head is the top of the star and the energetic point of *beauty*. As the Goddess draws this energy on you, it moves down your body to your right foot at the point of *devotion*, then up and over to your left hand and the point of *creativity*, across your body to your right hand at *desire*, to your left foot at *expression*, and back up to a close at the top of your head at *beauty*.

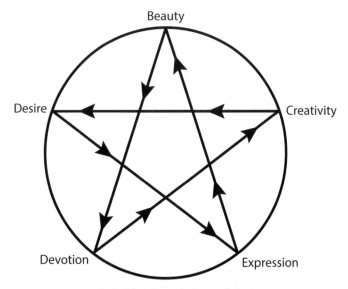

Figure 1: Beauty Pentacle

The flow of power to these energy centers, and how it moves in each of them, is only the first part of the process. Once you understand the flow and how each point works, then you start to unpack how the points work together, support each other, and the triangles of influence that the points have on each other.

The points of the pentacle are not just dots connecting one line to the next. Rather, they are energetic points. They are spheres of energy that you can open and close. When you are connected to your core worth, to your best self, to beauty, the spheres should spin, move, and glow. When you are not your best, when you are feeling disconnected, or struggling to find your joy, the energy spheres may be sluggish, cold, or closed up. This is how pentacles work as diagnostic tools. By running energy through them, you can discover where you may need to give yourself more love, attention, or beauty.

Once you have mastered the flow of energy from one point of the pentacle to the next, you have to put a circle around the star. The circle is made energetically by moving from one point to the next around the energy centers of the star in a deosil (or clockwise) direction. With the Beauty Pentacle this would be moving from *beauty* to *creativity* to *expression* to *devotion* to *desire*. When you are fully in balance, when you are connected to your own beauty and the beauty of the greater world, this energetic circle will form on its own without any pushing or prompting from you. This is part of the advanced work of the Beauty Pentacle. When you are integrated with the Beauty Pentacle, when it becomes a part of your breath, blood, and bone, the circle will appear.

This may develop easily, or it could take some practice. Until the outer circle appears on its own for you, you can run the circle yourself by visualizing or energetically moving the energy from one point to the next. Let the circle develop moving from point to point. Try running this circle first by shifting the energy around you in a deosil (or clockwise) direction and then try it widdershins (or counterclockwise). See what feels right for your body. See what feels like the truest expression of beauty for you. No one else can tell you what beauty looks or feels like, each of us has our own definition and relationship with beauty. And that will play out when you run the energy through your body.

Pentacle vs. Pentagram

Mathematically speaking, a *pentagram* is a five-pointed star and a *pentacle* is a five-pointed star with a circle around it. Spiritually and magickally speaking, a *pentagram* is a representation of the elements of life, and a *pentacle* is the elements of life working in harmony.

The energy of this work is a pentacle—not a pentagram. This is because the energy of the Beauty Pentacle runs through our bodies, but it is also all around us. It surrounds and holds us. We can look out and see it. It is both a part of us and outside of us. It is paradox.

When the Beauty Pentacle is in harmony, we are in balance with the power of it. The circle around the star is solid, strong, and visible. It is our working in harmony with beauty that makes it possible for it to form the circle.

Discernment

Your most powerful tool throughout the process of working with the Beauty Pentacle is discernment. Discernment is a strong ability to judge. It sounds so simple, but it is immensely powerful. Discernment is the most powerful tool a Witch or Pagan can possess. This is not about judging others, but rather, discernment is awareness of oneself using honest judgment and reflection. It is a tool for looking at your own motivations and progress. Judgment is not meant to be self-punishment or cruelty; self-discernment as in honesty and clarity.

As you develop a relationship with the Beauty Pentacle, it will be important to use your discernment on how the magick is working for you. You will need to engage with your discernment with every journaling process, exercise, and ritual. Check in with that tool over and over again. Trust it; it is powerful.

✦ ✦ ✦ CHECK-IN ✦ ✦ ✦

Draw a pentacle in your journal and write the points of the Beauty Pentacle on it. What are some of your first impressions and thoughts? Consider taking a few days before reading further and just focus on the overall pentacle. Write down any feelings that come through in your contemplation.

BEAUTY PENTACLE ENERGY

How the energy of the Beauty Pentacle looks and feels moving through your body will be unique. This pentacle doesn't have a specific color, viscosity, or intensity. The Beauty Pentacle is yours and will look and feel like you need it to.

Each point of the Beauty Pentacle stands alone, and yet, they also flow together. The energy centers of the pentacle fit together like puzzle pieces and interlock in certain ways. Trust how the pentacle looks and feels when you move the energy of it through your body. As you work with it longer, it may change color or flow; it may get thicker or thinner. Let this develop as it needs to without trying to force or control it.

DISCOVERING BEAUTY
Running the Beauty Pentacle

The first time you run the Beauty Pentacle through your body, give yourself plenty of time and space to have a full ritual experience. Find a place where you can be alone for twenty to thirty minutes. Turn off your phone and any other potential distractions. This working can be done with a group or as a solitary practitioner. For best results, record yourself reading the exercise and listen back to it.

Supplies: Black copal incense, fire-safe container, flowers, vase, large purple candle, image of something you find beautiful, something delicious to eat, and a lovely plate.

Set Up: Create an altar with a vase of flowers and the large purple candle. Place the image of something beautiful in front of the flowers. Then put your delicious food on the plate and set that on the altar. Place the black copal incense in a fire-safe container.

Ritual: Light the incense. As the smoke begins to curl up around you, lift up the incense burner and move it around your body. Allow the smoke of the incense to cleanse your spirit body. When that feels complete, set down the incense and smell the flowers. Give yourself plenty of time to take in the scent of the blossoms. When that feels complete, light the candle and take in the beauty of the candle's flame. Watch as it flickers and dances. When your senses have feasted on these simple forms of beauty, move on to the next part of the ritual.

Stand with your arms and legs spread—or lay on the floor with your arms and legs spread—making the shape of a star with your body. Take three long, slow, deep breaths. Allow yourself to become fully present in your body. Continue to breathe, allowing any distractions or lingering thoughts to clear away. Feel your breath and feel your connection to the earth below you.

Trance: Say the word "beauty" out loud three times. Feel the word "beauty" as it rolls across your tongue and palate. Feel how your mouth and lips move when you speak this word. Listen to the sound of it rumble through your head. Breathe deeply.

Let your thoughts begin to wander on to things that are beautiful. Allow your mind to recreate moments where you have been awestruck. Recall beautiful places you've been, beautiful moments you've witnessed, beautiful experiences you've had. Let these images fill your heart and allow your breath to fill your physical body with these images, feelings, and thoughts. Let this build up until you are thrumming with the power of beauty.

Take a moment to notice the color of this energy. What does it look like, feel like, smell like? What is the viscosity of the energy of beauty? Take your time with this exploration. There is no rush. (Pause.) When you feel ready, draw this energy up into the top of your head. Pull up the power of beauty from all your cells, allowing it to flow swiftly up to the top of your head. As this power moves, notice how fast or slow the energy is flowing. Is it thick and strong, effervescent, light, airy, or soft? Take note of how the energy wants to be in your body.

Let the power of beauty gather at the top of your head. We call this point "beauty." Repeat that word out loud: "beauty." Take a breath and connect into this energy sphere. Allow it to develop into a large ball of energy. Let the power of beauty in the energy center at the top of your head begin to spin and swirl. Take time to note any dark spots, holes, or stuck places in the sphere of beauty. Notice the color and thickness of this energy. Give yourself plenty of time and space to connect into this beauty ball of power. (Pause.) Let it build up until you feel that you can't hold it any longer in the beauty point.

The energy in the beauty point will begin to crest and overflow. Direct it down the right side of your body and into your right foot. We call this point "devotion." Repeat that word out loud: "devotion." Take a breath and let the power of this energy center build into a large energetic sphere at your right foot. Connect into the power of devotion. Notice how this energy sphere feels, looks, tastes, smells. Allow the energy of devotion to spin *and swirl, taking note of any dark spots, holes, or stuck energy. Give yourself plenty of time and space to connect into the ball of power that is devotion. (Pause.) Let this power grow and build until it starts to overflow.*

The built-up energy of devotion begins to overflow, moving up and across your body into your left hand. We call this point "creativity." Repeat that word out loud: "creativity." Take a breath and let the energy of this sphere awaken and spin, picking up speed. Connect into this power, this energy center, and notice the flow, color, and thickness. Take note if there are any holes or stuck energy here. How does creativity feel, move, and spin? Take plenty of time and space to connect into the ball of power that is creativity. (Pause.) Let this power grow and build until it starts to overflow.

The power of creativity flows onward, across your body, and into your right hand. We call this point "desire." Say this word out loud: "desire." Take a breath and let the power build here. Allow the energy center of desire to awaken, spin, and come alive. Notice if there are any holes, dark spots, or stuck energy in the sphere of desire. Take notice of how this energy center moves, spins, and feels. Allow plenty of time to connect into the power of desire. (Pause.) Let it grow and build until it overflows and crests, spilling outward.

The energy of desire flows down and across your body into your left foot. We call this point "expression." Say that word out loud: "expression." Take a breath and allow the power here to build into a sphere. The energy swirls and spins, awakening a ball of power. Take note of the flow here. Are there holes, stuck places, or any dark spots in the sphere of expression? (Pause.) Breathe into this point, feel the flow and the power, allowing it to build, crest, and overflow.

The power of expression flows out and upward, back into the top of your head where the pentacle is completed, coming to a rest at the energy sphere of beauty. Breathe into the living beauty pentacle that is your body. Notice how you feel, how the power flows, and what is coming up for you now. Breathe into the living beauty pentacle that is you. (Pause)

Focus the flow of energy through the body, naming each point out loud as it moves through you: beauty, devotion, creativity, desire, expression. Run this energy through your body again, increasing the speed from one point to the next. Allow your body to thrum with beauty. Keep running the pentacle, feeling the flow with ease from one point to the next. (Pause.) When you feel complete, when the pentacle feels alive in your body, stop running the energy of the Beauty Pentacle through you and let yourself just sit in the power of it. (Long pause.)

When you feel ready, slowly open your eyes.

Give yourself time and space to write down your experience and reactions. Make sure that you notice where the energy may have felt stuck or had holes and also where the flow was graceful and easy. Eat the delicious food off of your plate as you write down any thoughts to help you ground. This will be important information as you continue to work through the Beauty Pentacle.

CHAPTER 4

WORKING WITH THE BEAUTY PENTACLE

The Beauty Pentacle is an energetic tool to add into your personal spiritual arsenal. There are many ways to work with this tool, but as I've said before, I highly recommend letting your intuition and discernment guide you. There is no right or wrong, but know that the more you connect into the power of the Beauty Pentacle, the more it will inform and influence how you look at the world. The more you move this energy through your body and work on your blocks and shadows, the brighter you will shine. Beauty is everywhere, all the time.

RUNNING THE PENTACLE

The simplest and most effective way to incorporate the Beauty Pentacle into your practice is to "run" it. Move the energy through your body, taking time to connect with each of the five energy centers or points. At first, it is best to run the Beauty Pentacle on a daily basis to help deepen your connection to this power. Run the energy slowly, run the energy quickly, run the energy when you need to reconnect to beauty, run the energy when you've had a hard day, run the energy when you have seen something beautiful and you want to integrate it into your body. Run that pentacle. Take notes when you run the Beauty Pentacle, write down patterns you may notice, interesting or odd reactions, anything that feels important to connecting into this work.

Discovering Beauty
Daily Beauty Pentacle

For the next week, run the Beauty Pentacle every morning when you first wake up. Allow the power of the Beauty Pentacle to permeate your being. As it runs through your body, notice where you may feel obstacles, blocks, or stuck energy and breathe through them. How does running this energy through your body impact the rest of your day? Write your thoughts in your Beauty Pentacle journal.

In the following week, run the Beauty Pentacle midway through your day. No matter what you are doing, take ten to fifteen minutes to focus on the Beauty Pentacle. If you need to, set an alarm to help you remember. Again, notice where there may be obstacles or stuck energy and breathe through them. Write down your thoughts in your journal and take note of patterns that may, or may not, match your morning Beauty Pentacle routine.

During the third week, run the Beauty Pentacle right before you go to sleep. Take note of any blocks or resistance and breathe through them. Upon waking, write down any dreams, feelings, or images that come to you first thing. Take note of how the Beauty Pentacle may influence your day ahead and write that down too. Again, look at any similarities or differences from when you ran the pentacle in the morning and at midday.

THE ALTAR

Create a Beauty Pentacle altar that you can use while you work on incorporating the Beauty Pentacle into your life. The altar can also serve as a touchstone, a place where you can reconnect to the beauty around you when you are struggling.

An altar doesn't have to be a large space. Make it work for the space that you have. It could be a whole table, a small corner of a shelf, the top of an entertainment center, a desk drawer, or any other creative place you might be able to think of.

A beauty altar needs to be a place that gets used. Don't create an altar and then ignore it and let it fill with dust. Clean your altar on a weekly basis at least: dust it, burn incense on it, give offerings of fresh flowers, or whatever else you feel called to do. But make sure that you are actively working with this space.

On your altar, place images of things that you find beautiful, keep fresh flowers, put the purple candle from the exercise where you first ran the pentacle, and create a physical Beauty Pentacle to put down on your altar space. You might want to make a pentacle out of clay, find one made of metal, or just draw one on a piece of parchment. What is important is to have an image of the pentacle for you to look at when needed.

You will also need a mirror for this work, which I will go into more detail about in one of the next sections. When you create your beauty altar space, make sure that you leave room for this mirror. Keep in mind that your magickal mirror may be a hand-held mirror, a framed mirror, a mirror with a stand, or even a smaller loose craft mirror.

Add to your beauty altar whenever you find something inspiring or beautiful. It might be a picture, a stone, a written word, a flower, or anything that fills your heart with beauty.

Beauty Image

In my personal practice I use visual touchstones to help me key into what it is I want to bring into my life. As I work through the different points of the pentacle, I find images that call to that energy when I look at them. Primarily these images go on my altar, but you could also place these images on your workspace, bathroom mirror, the dashboard of your car, a Pinterest page, or anywhere you will regularly see them.

I encourage you to find images that speak to you of beauty. Cut out pictures from magazines, print things off of the internet, sort through oracle decks, take photos and print them out, and pick up random bits that you find out in the world. Put these items and images on your beauty altar and in places where you will see them often so they can remind you of the beautiful things in the world.

The Mirror

The magickal tool of the Beauty Pentacle is the mirror. The mirror shows you reflections. It can give you a clear glimpse into yourself, both your bright and hidden shadows. The mirror can reveal things you'd rather keep hidden. A mirror can open portals, connect you to ancestors or deities, and deflect negativity. It is a powerful tool.

As you work with the Beauty Pentacle, it will be important that you have your own magickal mirror. Ideally, your Beauty Pentacle mirror is a hand mirror that you don't mind decorating. What I believe works best is an inexpensive mirror that you can glue items to, draw on the handle of, write messages to yourself on (such as around the glass), and make into a beautiful work of art. However, a special mirror, family heirloom, or antique mirror can also work. Your mirror should be a traditional looking glass and not a black mirror.

Just like everything with the Beauty Pentacle, the most important thing about your Beauty Mirror is that it appeals to you. If a small mirror square is what you've got, use it! If you have an old, large antique mirror that you feel called to use, perfect! Use your discernment.

My magickal mirror is a pink plastic mirror that I found at a dollar store. It is very plain and basic, but I have consecrated it as a magickal tool. I have blessed it and listened carefully as it shared its name with me. I have decoupaged a beautiful image on the back and down the handle. Around the "glass," I have written words in permanent marker: "You are beautiful," "See beauty," and "Enjoy the view." It lives on my magickal altar and I use it when working the Beauty Pentacle and more.

The mirror on my altar has candles burned on top of its glass. I look at myself in it and speak blessings. I take it on hikes and use it to look at beautiful things. Every time I use it to see the reflection of something beautiful, it takes on some of the power of that beauty, making it stronger. It is also a portal for me to commune with one of my Fae allies. Your beauty mirror holds endless possibilities.

Ritual: Cleansing and Consecrating Your Beauty Mirror

This ritual is designed to take an ordinary mirror and bless it as a sacred ritual object for beauty. This ritual is best performed during a full moon and at night if possible. After the ritual is complete, you will need to wrap your mirror in black fabric and keep it in a safe place for the next month.

This ritual is written for a solitary practitioner but can also be modified for a group that wants to do the working together.

Supplies: Mirror, markers, items to decorate your mirror, sage or cedar, a bowl of salt water, a white candle, a bowl of soil, an athame, and a piece of black fabric large enough to wrap around your mirror.

Set Up: Create an altar with the mirror in the center; this could be your beauty altar or a space you create just for this ritual. Around your mirror place the sage or cedar, white candle, bowl of soil, and bowl of salt water. In front of you, place the athame. Nearby, or on the altar if possible, place all of the items that you have gathered for decorative purposes.

Ritual: Before you begin, take a cleansing bath. Add salts, herbs, flowers, candles, and anything that will help you sink into feeling beauty. You may also want to play soft music or burn incense. Make your bathroom look like a place where you would want to spend time. As you bathe, let the feelings of beauty sink into your skin. Get out of the tub, dry off, and dress in something simple and comfortable.

When you step in front of your altar, take a moment to breathe deeply. Give yourself some time and space to become fully present. Continue to take clear and focused breaths. With each breath, release anything unnecessary and let your awareness continue to come into the present moment. When you feel ready, pick up your athame.

Using your athame, visualize the shimmering, shining energy that comes from a quartz crystal. Visualize that shimmering power tucked deep in the earth. Use your athame to draw that glow up from the deep below. Direct that power to the north, flinging it out like a fishing line. Visualize that iridescent shimmering quartz energy spread and expand, moving both up and down.

Pointing your tool to the north, draw a pentacle in the air, silently calling in all the beauty of the earth. Turn and face the east, pushing the crystalline energy outward as you move. Facing the east, draw another pentacle, silently calling in all the beauty of air. Continue this expansion of crystal energy to the south and draw another pentacle, calling in the beauty of fire. Turn to the west, calling in the beauty of water. Turn again to the north, completing your circle.

Return to your altar and light the sage or cedar. Say this: *I call upon the spirit of air to join in my circle. Please bring the cool winds on a hot summer day. Please bless my circle with the sound of beautiful music. Please send laughter, whispers, and joyful conversations. Welcome, air.*

Light the white candle and say this: *I call upon the spirit of fire to join in my circle. Please bring the joyful flames of a bonfire. Please bless my circle with the warmth of a banked hearth. Please send heat, passion, and exciting adventures. Welcome, fire.*

Hold the bowl of salt water above your head and say this: *I call upon the spirit of water to join in my circle. Please bring the soothing comfort of a warm bath. Please bless my circle with a soft spring rain. Please send deep emotional connections, intuition, and holding hands. Welcome, water.*

Set down the bowl of salt water and pick up the bowl of soil. Say this: *I call upon the spirit of earth to join in my circle. Please bring the steady heartbeat of the ancestors. Please bless my circle with groundedness. Please send patience, calm, and the delicious smell of blossoms. Welcome, earth.*

If there is a deity that you regularly work with or want to call in to help you with the consecration of your beauty mirror, do this now. When calling deity into this ritual, speak from your heart and ask for their blessings and guidance while dressing and blessing your magickal mirror.

Now decorate your mirror. Let this process unfold as you feel called. Perhaps you play some music or sing while you create. Your decoration can be as complex or simple as you desire. And you don't have to complete your decorating in this one session. Your beauty mirror may take time to develop. Just do what feels right in the moment.

When you have finished decorating, run your mirror through the smoke of the sage or cedar. Say this: *With the blessings of air*. Run your mirror over the candle flame and say this: *With the blessings of fire*. Sprinkle your mirror with the salt water and say this: *With the blessings of water*. Lay your mirror down in the bowl of soil and say this: *With the blessings of earth*.

If you have called deity into your circle, now is the time to ask for their blessing in this work. Speak from your heart.

When complete, hold your mirror up to the moon. You may want to step outside, move to a window, or just hold your mirror up to the sky. It doesn't matter if the moon is visible; the energy of it is still present. Say this:

I call into this mirror the power of beauty.
Bestow into this mirror your grace.

I call into this mirror the power of devotion.
Bestow into this mirror your essence.

I call into this mirror the power of creativity.
Bestow into this mirror your spark.

I call into this mirror the power of desire.
Bestow into this mirror your passion.

I call into this mirror the power of expression.
Bestow into this mirror your bravery.

By the power of beauty, devotion, creativity, desire, and expression, I consecrate this mirror as a magickal tool, a lifeline to beauty, a reminder and reflector of the beauty that exists in the world and in me.

So mote it be.

Look at yourself in the mirror. See the beauty reflected back. Look at the reflection of the moon in the mirror. See the beauty reflected back. Use the mirror to show you beauty in and around your ritual space. See the beauty reflected back.

If there was a deity that you called into the circle, now is the time to thank them and bid them farewell.

Kiss the mirror and place it back on your altar and pick up the bowl of soil. Say this: *Thank you to the spirit of the earth. Thank you for joining my circle. I am grateful for your reflection of beauty. May we continue to walk together with patience, calm, and the delicious smell of blossoms. Hail and farewell, earth.*

Set down the bowl of soil and pick up the bowl of salt water. Say this: *Thank you to the spirit of water. Thank you for joining in my circle. I am grateful for your reflection of beauty. May we continue to walk together with emotional connection, intuition, and holding hands. Hail and farewell, water.*

Set down the bowl of salt water and blow out the candle flame. Say this: *Thank you to the spirit of fire. Thank you for joining in my circle. I am grateful for your reflection of beauty. May we continue to walk together with heat, passion, and exciting adventures. Hail and farewell, fire.*

Put out the sage or cedar if it is still burning and say this: *Thank you to the spirit of air. Thank you for joining in my circle. I am grateful for your reflection of beauty. May we continue to walk together with laughter, whispers, and joyful conversations. Hail and farewell, air.*

Pick up your athame and open the circle you created. Starting in the north, use your athame to break open the pentacle you put there. Do this by piercing through the energetic bubble and visualize it shattering. Turn towards the west, break open the pentacle you placed there, and turn to the south. Repeat this pattern all the way around the circle until you get back to the north.

Clap your hands three times. The work is done.

Beauty Potions and Supplies

In this section, I offer some formulas for sprays, oils, herbs, and stones that can be used to enhance your work with the Beauty Pentacle. Using items that are known to enhance awareness, bring forth beauty, and make the wearer feel more beautiful will help you incorporate the Beauty Pentacle more easily.

There are also a couple of cleansing mixes that can be incorporated into your daily or weekly practices. The cleansing mixes are included to help you prepare the temple that is your body before stepping into ritual or magickal space.

With any of the following recipes, please don't use any ingredient if you are allergic. Always spot test with a new essential oil before putting it on your body and never ingest an essential oil. They are concentrated and can harm you! If you aren't sure about an allergic response, don't use it. Better safe than sorry.

Oils

An oil can be used as a perfume and worn every day or, alternatively, oils can be used as a spiritual anointing oil, only worn during ritual or spiritual workings. Oils can also be used to anoint spiritual supplies, candles, your beauty mirror, or sacred objects. With all of the oil mixture formulas you will need a base carrier oil. The best options for a base oil are jojoba, almond, or grapeseed oil. Create the essential oil mixture first, following the directions below, and then add in the carrier oil to fill up the rest of the container. The carrier oil should be added at a three to one ratio of any essential oils added to the mixture.

BEAUTY OIL
3 parts basil
3 parts rose perfume
2 parts rose geranium
1 part patchouli

DEVOTION OIL
3 parts cedar
3 parts frankincense
1 part lotus

CREATIVITY OIL
3 parts ginger
1 part juniper
1 part lemongrass

DESIRE OIL
3 parts cardamom
3 parts rose

1 part cinnamon
1 part vanilla

EXPRESSION OIL
3 parts jasmine
2 parts rosemary
1 part benzoin

ANOINTING OIL
5 parts sandalwood
3 drops myrrh
2 drops cinnamon
1 drop sweet orange

Sprays

A beauty spray could also be called a smokeless incense. It can be used on your body, on your altar, or on your mirror as a way to add beauty blessings and connect back into the Beauty Pentacle. Sprays are made with an alcohol and water base with essential oils added in.

SELF-LOVE ELIXIR SPRAY
1 part alcohol
1 part water
1 tumbled rose quartz
10 drops rose perfume essential oil
5 drops cinnamon essential oil
5 drops gardenia essential oil

CLARITY SPRAY
1 part alcohol
1 part water
5 drops orange blossom essential oil

5 drops mugwort essential oil
5 drops lemongrass essential oil

PEACE SPRAY
1 part alcohol
1 part water
10 drops lavender essential oil
5 drops chamomile essential oil
5 drops cedar essential oil

CLEANSING SPRAY
1 part alcohol
1 part water
10 drops lemon essential oil
5 drops cedar essential oil
5 drops sage essential oil

CLEANSING HERB MIX
1 part hyssop
1 part bay leaf
1 part lemongrass

SALT SCRUB
2 cups kosher salt
1 tablespoon almond oil
5 drops sage essential oil
5 drops lemon essential oil

Herbs

There are several herbs that help open you up to beauty. These herbs and plants can be used in a variety of ways. Making tisanes, washes, burning the herbs, incorporating them into food, and growing and picking the plants are all ways that herbs can connect you into beauty. Many of these herbs are used to "promote" beauty, meaning to make yourself more beautiful. But I truly feel that the more we can connect to beauty, the more beautiful we will feel automatically. Let these herbs fuel your beauty awareness and make you feel more beautiful. Here are my favorite herbs and plants for working with the Beauty Pentacle:

Avocado: Carry an avocado pit in your pocket to help open your eyes to the beauty around you.

Catnip: Often used in spells to bring in love, happiness, and beauty. Catnip can be carried in a mojo bag, sachet, or ingested.

Flax: Keep your pocket filled with a handful of flax to connect you into the energy of beauty and to be seen as more beautiful.

Maidenhair: Creating a tisane (herbal tea) with maidenhair and then using the water as a face wash will bring beauty. It can also help with love and gracefulness.

Sweet pea: Wearing sweet peas will help you to develop solid relationships with people and see their beauty. It can also bring out your courage and truth telling.

Stones

Working with stones can be a great way to shift your energy and incorporate more beauty into your life. There are many stones, gems, and crystals that help to lift moods, bring joy, and open our eyes to the beauty that is all around and within us. Here are my favorite stones for the Beauty Pentacle:

Emerald has been called the seeker of love and the revealer of truth. It is an excellent stone to work with when looking to increase your self-love and acceptance. It can help to grow self-esteem and release negative messages about yourself from the past. It has been revered for thousands of years as a stone of beauty.

Lepidolite is known as the stone of transition because it can help you to release old patterns and step into the next phase of your life. It is a stone of emotional healing, allowing stress and depression to lift and lighten. This stone helps to solidify independence, fostering self-love and intuitive trust.

Orange Calcite is an uplifting stone. It can help you to connect, or reconnect, to life force. This stone brings happiness and joy, allowing you to clear blocks of depression and see beauty in the world around you.

Selenite is the ultimate cleansing stone. It is self-cleaning and doesn't require some of the cleansing processes that other stones might need from time to time. This stone clears negative energy from your body, rooms, other stones, and virtually anything. It's an excellent stone to keep on a beauty altar to keep refreshing the energy.

Sunstone contains the power of the sun within it. It brings joy, happiness, and it awakens connections to the greater world. An excellent stone for abundance. Sunstone brings forth abundance in all forms, opening you to receive all the blessings that you desire.

Unakite is a stone of relationships. It can help to heal complicated issues, allowing the beauty of connection to shine through. It helps to alleviate bad habits and betrayal. This is a stone of beauty, helping people to reconnect to the beauty in the world.

Glamour

The concept of glamour is one that has deep roots in Witch-craft. Glamour, glamoury, and putting on a glamour are all terms for the type of spell where you shift your external appearance. This is not done with makeup or prosthetics but with magick. Many Hollywood movies about Witchcraft have explored glamour magick. In the movie *The Craft*, one of the main characters masters this art and changes her outward appearance to look like another character. In the Disney movie *The Little Mermaid*, the sea witch changes her appearance to look like a beautiful young woman in order to enchant the unsuspecting prince. Glamour in the movies is portrayed as a working to totally transform the way you look, but just like most things magickal, it doesn't really work like that in real life.

Glamour works on an internal process. A true glamour shifts your personal energy internally, making it perceptible from an external level. It's the ultimate magickal "fake it 'til you make it" type of spellcraft. In order for a glamour to be successful, you need full faith and trust that what you've created is perceptible to others. A glamour must have some basis in reality. Pulling a glamour of fully developed feathered wings or purple skin is highly unlikely to manifest.

A solid glamour is really advanced spellwork. It may be easy to put one on, but it takes a lot of practice to hold a glamour for a significant amount of time. If your focus or concentration wavers, the glamour will shake off too.

Glamour relates to the Beauty Pentacle because beauty work is twofold. It is how we look at the world *and* how we look at ourselves. This concept of beauty is not about the over-culture's beauty ideal. This is not about how much you "measure up" to the airbrushed covers of magazines, what gender you are, what size clothes you wear, what hair style you have, or what the mainstream opinion of you might be. It is possible to feel beautiful and enjoy your own beauty no matter what your physical circumstances.

If you are unable to look at yourself and see beauty or feel beautiful, then you have some work to do. Every single person on this planet is beautiful. We are each a unique and special being. Each of us has a duty to honor that beauty, see it, revel in it, and flaunt it. If you find it challenging to stare into your own eyes for any significant amount of time, I challenge you to look at yourself in your beauty mirror every day until it becomes easy.

BEAUTIFUL WILD

Modern people are suffering from a serious and pernicious illness. It is the fallacy of disconnection. We live in a fantasy world that we are alone and must trudge through life making things happen all on our own. As a culture, we are disconnected from each other, we are disconnected from the land, and we are disconnected from our own wild natures.

This is especially true for Americans who are taught that we have to "pick ourselves up by our bootstraps." Everything we need can be purchased online. We never need to leave our houses or interact with other people at all if we don't choose to. This is a major problem.

By stepping into the wild, being in liminal spaces, feeling the wind on our faces and the sun on our skin, we awaken the beauty within. Beauty is recognition that we are wild. Beauty is awareness that we are of the land. Beauty is remembering that we are all connected. Beauty is pain; beauty is love. It is grief and wellness; it is hope and prayer. Beauty is honesty and vulnerability.

Beauty is knowing your neighbor and the folks who sell vegetables at the farmer's market. Beauty is understanding that the power stays on due to a long and complicated set of connections to and with other people.

Doing this work means that you will have to step outside of your home. You may be called to take a walk or go to a wild place. This work will ask you to connect with other people and remember the precious connection that humans have with each other. This is a vital part of the Beauty Pentacle.

However, not all of us have the same levels of physical ability. If a walk in a wild place isn't possible for your body, then modify for what is possible for your body. If going to a wild place isn't possible, find a beautiful view outside of your own windows. If the only human connection you can handle is through the internet, then honor those connections. Don't let anything stand in your way.

The more we honor and connect to the fragile and complicated state of being alive, the more we live in beauty and walk with the Beauty Pentacle.

Developing a Beginner's Mind

The most important part of this working is to maintain a sense of wonder. Do you currently find wonder out in the world? Can you appreciate something without having to name it, label it, or have a scientific explanation of its existence? A sense of wonder is looking at something with fresh eyes. Letting the thing you are looking at be just what it is. You don't need to know what type of tree that is in order to find it beautiful, awesome, or inspiring.

A sense of wonder can also be called *beginner's mind*. I've been writing, creating, and helping to lead ritual for over twenty-five years. I've participated in hundreds of rituals. I can spot a "mistake" in a ritual from a mile away. I can tell when someone missed their cue, when someone went longer than they were supposed to, or when something fell flat. This is a helpful skill when planning a ritual or helping to facilitate one, but it really sucks when trying to be a participant.

There have been times that I struggled to pull myself out of the critical mode, which only served to make me a terrible ritual participant. There have been times when I couldn't close the curtain and let the mystery take over. I was too busy watching the ritual unfold as if I was a producer of the magick.

A dear friend and mentor suggested that during the next ritual I attended I should put on a beginner's mind. She encouraged me to pretend that this was all new for me. She threw down the gauntlet, telling me that I should fake it 'til I make it. Could I step in and release my critic and give over to the mystery?

I had to prepare for this, but I did it. Before leaving my house, I settled into the beginner's mind. I let myself be filled with a sense of wonder. When I noticed that critic voice starting to creep back in, I just said thank you, but your services aren't needed right now. I found myself enjoying a ritual for the first time in a year. It was magickal!

This sense of wonder, this beginner's mind, can help us to shift out of negative patterns or boredom and back into a place of awe and wonder with parts of our everyday life.

Part Two

The
Points

Chapter 5
Beauty

In the early days of spring, a meadow is covered in a carpet of bluebells. The lush green and delicate blue from the leaves and petals stretches out as far as the eye can see. There is a faint droning buzz in the air as bees alight on one soft blossom after another. The breeze flows past carrying the sweet scent of the fragrant flowers. The beauty is captivating.

A small child sits quietly on the floor with a little fluffy kitten in her hands. The kitten mewls and meows, its little pin-like claws poking into the bare flesh of her little leg. She cries silent tears of joy because she adores the furry creature beyond all measure. The beauty is heart wrenching.

The first breath of a newborn baby. The croak of a raven floating on outstretched wings through a forest. Wild horses running freely through plains of grass. A family reunited after being separated by a wall. A humpback whale breeching. The twinkling lights of the city. The shining swath of stars blasting through the night sky outside of the reaches of light pollution. The kindness of neighbor looking after neighbor. A dog waiting for his soldier owner to return. The countless number of people who put themselves in harm's way to help another living creature.

Beauty is truly everywhere. We don't have to look very hard to see it. Beauty makes our hearts burn with a joy that fills our eyes with tears. Beauty restores our faith in humanity. Beauty is our humanity. Beauty is the mystery of the world, and yet, that mystery is oh so simple.

Beauty is the overarching power of this pentacle. We start with the point of beauty and the energy center that resides at the top of our heads. This energy center is where we connect to our god-selves. This is the location of our higher self or the crown chakra. This is the part of our body that connects us to something bigger than ourselves. It is through this connection to our god-self that we can open our inner eye and begin to see beauty everywhere we look. The divine knows that the world is beautiful; we only need open our awareness to be in alignment with that reality.

Yes, the Beauty Pentacle is about seeing beauty out in the world and using that as a fuel for power, happiness, and focus, but it's not solely an outward focus. The Beauty Pentacle also asks us to take a good look at ourselves, the skin that we're in, and see the beauty there too. We can't truly see the beauty in one without seeing the beauty in the other.

In facing the energy of the beauty point of the pentacle, we must also face the dominant culture's expectations of beauty. Because of our over-culture, the word "beauty" may trigger feelings of not being enough, not meeting standards, or facing unfair judgments. We may find ourselves "in" or "out" of alignment with these superficial standards. The truth is that all people struggle with beauty—with feeling beautiful. This is solely due to outside, external influences, and most of those influences are total crap.

Beauty may be an uncomfortable or triggering word for some of us. Beauty may be a word that you have never felt a connection to within yourself, or you may have never been interested in connecting to beauty. You may not feel like you can call yourself beautiful because of your gender, appearance, work, age, status, ethnicity, or a million other over-culture messages. It could be that none of the labels you identify with allow for you to connect into beauty.

I'm going to tell you something really important right now, and I want you to pay close attention. You. Are. Beautiful. Absolutely, one hundred percent. You are beautiful. It is important that you know that. It may not be possible to feel that, or own that, all of the time. But you need to know it; you need to feel it in the core of your being.

Figure 2: Beauty Sigil

PERSONAL DEVELOPMENT

The following exercises are to help you work through your relationship with beauty on a personal level. How do you feel more beautiful? How do you connect to your own beauty? How do you work to connect more with the beauty around you?

> ### ✦ ✦ ✦ CHECK-IN ✦ ✦ ✦
> ### BEAUTY
> How do you feel about the skin you're in? Do you feel like a beautiful being? Do you appreciate and value your physical body, perceived flaws and all? How does it feel to think of yourself as a beautiful being? Write about these feelings openly and honestly.

DISCOVERING BEAUTY
Look at Yo'self

The following exercise is meant to help you begin your connection to beauty with intention. This working should help you feel the connection between your own beauty and the power of the Beauty Pentacle.

Find a time and space where you can be undisturbed for at least thirty minutes. Have your journal handy to write down anything important or interesting as it pops up for you. You may want to set your space to help you feel more focused and grounded. This might include soft music, incense, or candles, but no set up is necessary beyond having your journal and beauty mirror ready.

Take a moment to breathe into your body. Breathe slowly and intentionally, allowing each breath to move into and through your body. Start by sending a breath into your toes and feet. Let each inhale be cleansing and comforting—the gift of air to your precious body. Continue to breathe slowly, filling up your body with that breath, letting it build up into your legs, filling your belly, awakening your rib cage and spine. Let your breath fill your arms and hands and fingers. Allow your breath to fill your neck and head, leaving you cleansed and clear.

When you feel fully present and clear, pick up your beauty mirror and look at yourself. Really look. Take your time with this process. When you start to focus on something that you don't like, a piece of yourself that you might consider a flaw, send a blessing breath to that part of yourself. Shift your focus on to something that you love about yourself, something beautiful, and breathe a blessing into that part of yourself. Continue to do this process of flaw and beauty, offering a breath each time you see another piece of yourself in the mirror.

Hold your own gaze and take note of how this feels. Is this comfortable or uncomfortable? For some folks this will be an easy and welcome process, while others may find this very difficult or triggering. Feel the feelings that come through, but don't drop your gaze from the mirror. If you want to smile or wink at yourself, do it! If you want to cry or rage, do it! But hold your focus by continuing to look at yourself in your beauty mirror.

Continue this process for thirty minutes. When you are done, say to yourself, "You are beautiful," and set down your beauty mirror. Spend some time writing in your journal about how this experience went for you.

Discovering Beauty
⬿ Making Rose Water ⬾

Roses are often connected to beauty and luxury. Roses appeal on many sensual levels: sight, scent, touch, and appearance. Creating rose water can be turned into a ritual for your own relationship to beauty.

Where I live, roses bloom twice a year, once in the spring and again in the fall. This exercise can only be done during these times of the year. Get out and go for a walk. You will want to be able to pick rose petals while you walk (with permission, of course). This may require you to head to a park, garden, or neighborhood that has lots of roses. You will also need a bag or basket for the rose petals that you pick.

As you walk, take note of the beauty around you. It doesn't matter if you are in a rural, suburban, or urban environment; find something beautiful while you walk. Let all of your senses take in the world around you.

As you find roses, take time to smell them, look at them, and enjoy all of their beauty. Before you pick anything, make sure you ask the plant for permission. Tell the plant that you will be creating a rose water to honor the beauty in the world and ask if it would be willing to be a part of that. Wait a moment for an answer. This may be clear and obvious or subtle, but only proceed to pick petals if you have been given an affirmative answer. If the plant gives you a "no," move on to another rose bush.

Pick only a few petals at a time. Feel the softness of the flower petals between your fingers. Smell the richness of the blossoms. Take your time with this process. You will need at least three cups of rose petals. Thank each rose as you go.

When you get home, rinse the petals with lukewarm water and then put the petals in a large pot. Fill the pot with enough water to just cover the petals. Breathe deeply and remember all of the beauty that you witnessed on your walk. Let your body fill up with the touch, feel, and scent of each rose that you picked. When you are full of this energy, run the Beauty Pentacle through your body and then use the first two fingers of your dominant hand to draw the Beauty Pentacle over the pot of petals.

On low heat, bring the water to a simmer for thirty minutes, or until the petals have lost most of their color. Strain off the water into a clear glass container. This is concentrated rose water. Draw the Beauty Pentacle over the top of the container and say this:

Blessed with beauty
Blessed with grace
Sweet scent of rose
A kiss upon my face

I charge this water
With beauty and love
May it bless all it touches
Like a gift from above

Beauty
Devotion
Creativity
Desire
Expression

By the power of three times three
As I will it so mote it be

To use, dilute one tablespoon of the concentrate into one cup of water. This can be used as a bath additive, a refresher spray, or as a perfume. The water will only be good for a few days unless you add a preservative. Alcohol works best for this.

Add one part water, one part alcohol, and one tablespoon rose water to make a spray that will last for several weeks. Use it as a beauty blessing any time it is needed.

✦ ✦ ✦ CHECK-IN ✦ ✦ ✦
WHAT'S BEEN BEAUTIFUL?

Every day for the next month, write down something beautiful that you saw or experienced. This could be a moment, a view you saw, something delicious you ate, or any other thing that struck you during your day. What's been beautiful?

Ritual: Gratitude Body Blessing

The state of the skin you're in doesn't matter. Your body does a lot for you. The following ritual is a way to connect to yourself and your body. This is a ritual for honoring your skin and giving a blessing to the vessel that holds your life force and spirit.

Supplies: Full-length mirror, anointing oil (your own or the appropriate oil from pages 59 and 60), massage oil or lotion, two large red or white candles, and a vase of flowers.

Set Up: Put the full-length mirror in a place where you can be undisturbed and alone for forty-five minutes to an hour. Make sure wherever you set up your mirror you are able to see your full body when you stand in front of it. Set the vase of flowers nearby along with the anointing oil. Put a candle on either side of the mirror.

Ritual: Set up your space while singing or playing music, keep
   the music playing throughout the ritual. Take a cleansing bath
   in whichever way that you like best. After you are dry, light the
   candles and stand naked in front of the mirror.

Take some time to look at your reflection. Do this without judgment. Look at the fullness of your body, the blessing and miracle
it is. Look at your scars, stretch marks, hair, bumps, lumps, dim-
ples, spots, and wrinkles. Look at what you love, what is lovely,
interesting, unique, special, and you. Turn around and peek over
your shoulder at the back of your body. Take in the part of yourself that you rarely see.

   Let yourself experience the feelings that come up throughout
this process. You may want to cry, or laugh, or sing, or roar. All of
the feelings that come up are good. Give yourself plenty of time
to express them as they appear.

   When you feel ready, take the massage oil and rub your feet.
You may need to sit on a blanket or chair to do this. Rub your
feet, showing your gratitude for all they do. Rub your feet, giving
thanks for all the steps that they take and how they swiftly carry
your body from place to place. Modify this as needed if you use a
wheelchair or have a prosthetic appendage. Honor the work and
beauty of the body you have.

   Let your hands move up your body, rubbing any sore muscles,
tight spots, and stiff places as you go. Show appreciation to your
body. Show your skin, muscles, bones, and ligaments thanks for
all the hard work they do; pamper yourself.

   Again, you may feel called to cry, laugh, or sing. Emotions
may build up and spill over. Let them. Let yourself feel and express whatever comes up for you as it comes up.

When you feel ready, pick up the anointing oil, put some of it in your hands, and anoint your feet one at a time. As you anoint your feet, say this: *Bless these feet that walk my own unique sacred path.*

Anoint each of your knees in turn. As you do, say this: *Bless these knees that kneel at the sacred altars of my life.*

Anoint the spot right above your natural pubic line with the oil and say: *Bless my sex that creates beauty.*

Anoint the center of your chest with the oil and say: *Bless my heart, formed with love and expressing love.*

Anoint your third eye with the oil and say: *Bless my sight, which leads my path.*

Finally, kiss your reflection in the mirror and say: *Bless my lips, which speak the sacred words, including my name.*

Stand before the mirror fully anointed. Look at your reflection and say: *Blessed be this creature of beauty.*

Put your hands in a prayer position and bow to your reflection, looking yourself in the eyes. Take some time to sit in silence. Just be. When you feel ready, journal or continue your blessing by eating something sumptuous. Give yourself the space to slowly come back into your regular life; move slowly and deliberately.

Welcome back.

DISCOVERING BEAUTY
◎◟ Beauty Cloak Trance ◞◎

Creating an object on the astral plane can impact you on the physical one. One way to bolster your own feelings around beauty is through the creation of an astral beauty cloak that you can use in your regular life. You can choose to keep this item with you at all times or put it on when you are about to step into an important moment.

This is a trance exercise that is best done alone. Find a time and place where you can be undisturbed for thirty minutes. Record yourself reading this trance ahead of time and play it back for the working. Sit or lie down as comfortably as you can.

Trance: Take three long and deep breaths. With each breath feel the edges of your body. Allow yourself to sink into this place. As your breathing continues, you find yourself surrounded by a thick mist. This mist is warm and comforting. It surrounds your body, gently lifting you up higher and higher. You float along weightless, surrounded by a warm, thick cloud. The cloud easily holds and carries you. You float along comfortable and carried. (Pause.)

The cloud begins to sink down, bringing you lower and lower until you feel your feet touch down on solid ground. The mist begins to slowly dissipate, and as it does you see a large wardrobe in front of you. The wardrobe is massive and wooden, with one intricately carved door in the center that flashes with an otherworldly glow.

Take a breath and open the door.

Inside the door, floating perfectly in the center of the opening, is a spectacular cloak. This cloak is luscious, beautiful, immaculate, and luxurious. The cloak totally appeals to your aesthetic. Take some time to really examine it. Look at the cut of it and the color and type of the fabric. Take in any embroidery or embellishments on the cloak. Reach out and feel the texture of the fabric. As you touch the cloak, you can also smell it. A fragrance wafts off of the cloak that fills your heart and makes you smile. The cloak seems to shimmer with magick. (Pause.)

This is your beauty cloak. If you were to put it on, it would become a part of you. It makes you show up as your best and brightest self. This magickal cloak will also show others how beautiful you are. It shows the truth of your beauty. Wearing this cloak brings forward effects that can be seen in the regular waking world. When you come here to this wardrobe and put on the cloak, other people in your life will be able to see the change in you.

Take a moment to lift this beauty cloak up and out of the wardrobe. Behind it you see a mirror. Place the cloak around your shoulders. Feel the weight of it on your body. Look into the mirror and see your reflection with the cloak on you. See how you glow with beauty when the cloak sits on your shoulders. It brings out your most beautiful characteristics. Let yourself glow. Notice what this feels like. (Pause.)

Suddenly, the cloak begins to absorb into your skin. It is warm, comfortable, and clearly belongs to you and only you. The process of the cloak sinking into you feels like the stroke of a feather across your skin. As the cloak absorbs, you know that at any moment when you need to feel more beautiful you can activate the power of this garment. Any time you need to remember that you are beautiful, you can return to this wardrobe and glance at your beautiful reflection in the mirror. This is another place where you can remember your beauty. (Pause.)

Close the door of the wardrobe. As you do, the mist returns, surrounding you in its warm embrace. The mist surrounds you and begins to lift you up higher and higher. The mist carries you swiftly and easily, holding you strong and solid. The mist begins to descend, moving lower and lower, setting you down gently in your body.

Take a moment to feel the edges of your body. Notice as your edges become more firm and solid. Breathe deeply and take a moment to feel what it is to be in your body at this time and at this place. As you feel ready, slowly open your eyes. Use the palms of your hands to tap your edges and say your name out loud three times.

Take some time to write down anything important or interesting from your trance process. If you feel so called, draw your cloak in your journal, making sure to include all of the details that you discovered in your exploration.

DISCOVERING BEAUTY
⟡ Daily Mirror Blessing ⟡

As you dive into your connection with the Beauty Pentacle, it is important that you take steps on a daily basis to hone your relationship to and with beauty. The following is a daily practice.

Every day look at your reflection in your beauty mirror. Look at your reflection for as long as you can. Notice all of your features. The things you love, the things you hate, the things that are changing; notice them all and send each of them a blessing. Spend at least ten minutes a day looking at your own reflection with a heart full of love. Find at least one thing that is beautiful. To end the working, tell yourself, "You are beautiful."

✦ ✦ ✦ CHECK-IN ✦ ✦ ✦
YOU ARE BEAUTIFUL

Get your journal and write the words "I am beautiful." Use the rest of the page to free write whatever comes up for you with these three words.

DISCOVERING BEAUTY
Mirror Glamour

Beauty is something we want to nurture, and beauty can help us feel more solid and strong throughout the day. When we feel in alignment with what we consider beautiful it can help to improve our mood. When we are in alignment with beauty it is easier to achieve our goals and step into the limelight. Beauty becomes an accessory that we put on. This accessory makes us bolder and braver. It gives us the power we might otherwise feel we lack. The confidence from owning this power brings more confidence, which calls success easily.

There will be days that you just don't have it in you, you feel run down, or you are off your game. This is the perfect opportunity to use your beauty mirror as a tool for shifting that energy and building you up through the power of beauty.

Hold your mirror in your hand, but don't look into it. Rather, take a moment to feel what it would be like if you were totally on your game, feeling strong and confident. Let yourself fill up with the glow of that power, and then look at yourself in your beauty mirror.

See yourself strong and confident. See yourself exactly as you would look if you felt that confidence inside yourself. Breathe into that feeling and really see it. Set down your mirror and go about your day fully charged with beauty.

✦ ✦ ✦ CHECK-IN ✦ ✦ ✦
BEAUTIFUL STRANGER

Pull out your journal and complete the following statements:

- The most beautiful thing I have ever seen is …
- I notice the beauty in the world by …
- Calling myself beautiful makes me feel …
- When I see something breathtaking, my body reacts by …
- When I see something breathtaking, my emotional reaction is …
- Beauty is …

If you are feeling exceptionally brave, consider posting your responses on social media and encouraging your friends to fill in their answers to these statements too. The more we share beauty with others and engage in these conversations, the more the doors to beauty are opened.

DISCOVERING BEAUTY
Beauty Battery

Sometimes, no matter how hard you try, you just can't muster any connection to the power of beauty. There will be times when you are low, sad, stuck, or just not feeling it. That's okay; it's all part of being human. But there will be times that you need to be your best and brightest even when you aren't feeling your connection to the flow.

The following working needs to be done when you are at the height of your power, when you are feeling your best self. If you can coordinate your beauty power peak with a full moon, that's even better. The goal is to take your beauty power peak moment and store some of that power for future use when you are struggling to feel that connection. It's charging up a beauty battery.

Of course, just like any other battery, it will need a recharge at times. Don't take your beauty battery for granted. The process to recharge it is the same as the process for the initial ritual charging.

Supplies: You will need a piece of jewelry or an article of clothing to ritually charge with beauty, a bowl of salt water, a bowl of spring water, your favorite incense, earth from your favorite place (sand, soil, or rocks), a crystal, several candles, an athame, an image that evokes the feeling of beauty within you, a bottle or cup of rose water, your beauty mirror, delicious sweet foods, and your favorite drink.

Set Up: Create an altar. You could use your beauty altar or put together a different space. On this altar, place all of the supplies listed in the above section with your piece of jewelry or article of clothing in the center of the other items. Make sure that the image of beauty can be easily seen. Take your time creating this space. Make sure that you find it beautiful to look at.

When you are finished, take a cleansing bath. If a bath isn't possible, take a cleansing shower. Wash your body, but also wash your spirit body. Take time to release what no longer serves you down the drain. Sometimes a salt scrub can help you with this process. When you are done with your bath, anoint yourself with your favorite oil or perfume.

Ritual: Step up to your altar and take several deep breaths. Center yourself, feeling the edges of your body. Feel your feet on the floor and take time to honor the connection between you, the earth, and the sky. Breathe this into your body.

When you feel ready, light the candles and the incense. Take a moment to notice how the light and smoke changes the feeling of the room around you. Look at the glow of the candlelight and the cloaking magick of the incense smoke. Does this make the room feel more beautiful, more magickal, or energetically shifted?

Pick up your athame and touch the tip of it to the image of beauty that you have placed on your altar. Allow the feeling of beauty to fill up your athame with a thrumming lavender color. When the athame is full of lavender energy, move to the north and send a tendril of that energy out, creating a barrier between you and the outside world.

Turn to face the east, releasing more of that lavender energy as you turn. Visualize the lavender color spreading up and down as you move, creating a bubble around you. Keep turning, moving south, then west, then back to the north, completing the circle. Finally, hold your athame above you, sealing off any open spots. Then point your athame down to the ground below you and fill up any holes or weak spots. Set the athame down on your altar.

Call in any godds, ancestors, or allies that you want to join you in this work. Do this by speaking from the heart.

Pick up the item that you want to imbue with beauty. Dip your fingers into the bowl of salt water and sprinkle the item with the salt water to cleanse that item and prepare it to take on beauty. Run the object through the incense smoke and say this: *By the air that carries my sacred words.* Move the item over the candle flame, being cautious to not burn the item and say this: *By the fire that carries my passions.* Sprinkle the item with the spring water and say this: *By the water of my living blood.* Set the item on the soil, stone, or crystal and say: *By the earth that is my body.*

Anoint yourself and the item with the rose water. Let yourself feel beautiful. Feel what it is to be at the top of your game: strong, confident, graceful, powerful, at your best.

Set the beauty image flat on your altar and put your ritual object on top of it. Take some time to run the Beauty Pentacle through your body until you feel yourself full of beauty. Let the pentacle continue to move through you until you are overflowing with the power of it. When you feel that you cannot hold onto the power of it any longer, place your hands on the object and release the energy of the Beauty Pentacle into the object. Chant the points of the pentacle as you release the power: *beauty, devotion, creativity, desire, expression.* Continue to chant these words, letting the energy build up. When it reaches capacity, let the power rush through you, moving through your body, out your hands, and into the object you are charging with beauty.

When the energy is fully released, put the item on. Notice how it feels to be fully in your power, fully in your beauty. Pick up your beauty mirror and look at yourself. See how powerful and beautiful you look. Carefully take in the glow of the object that you are wearing. How does this object look as it is fully charged?

Place your beauty mirror back on your altar along with your newly charged object. Open sacred space, and enjoy your food and drink.

Put the object on anytime you need a boost in confidence or personal power. This object is now a beauty battery that can help you recharge when you need it the most. Anytime you feel called, repeat the ritual to recharge the object for future use.

Occasionally check on this item to make sure that the charge is still at full capacity. If you notice it doesn't feel as strong or starts to weaken, repeat this ritual to fill it back up.

INTERPERSONAL DEVELOPMENT

The following exercise is designed to help you work through your relationship with beauty and your relationship with others. How do your feelings about beauty impact how you move through the world? Can awareness of your blocks with beauty heal some of the challenges you may be experiencing?

DISCOVERING BEAUTY
Forms of Beauty Contemplation

Understanding how you feel about beauty in different forms can help you step into a more balanced relationship with beauty. The following exercise is a series of meditation contemplations to help you explore your preconceived notions on beauty. Do this contemplation process now and then again in a few months. Compare how your feelings may have shifted after working with the Beauty Pentacle for a longer period of time.

Set Up: You will need about thirty minutes where you can comfortably lie or sit undisturbed. If you are doing this meditation alone, record yourself reading it and play it back. If you are doing it with a group, have one person read the trance for you. Have a glass of water and your journal close at hand for afterwards.

Trance: Get comfortable and begin to slow down. Allow your body to relax and focus on the ease and flow of your breathing. Don't attempt to force your breath, just let it come as it wants to. As you breathe allow your edges to soften. With each breath, your edges continue to expand, grow, and release. (Pause.)

From this place of expanded awareness, consider the word "beauty." Consider the external pressures of what it means to be beautiful. How do you feel about your own physical beauty? Do you feel pressured by the over-culture's expectation of beauty? Sit with the idea of external beauty and see where this shows up in your body. Breathe through any tightness or difficulty. (Pause.)

Run the Beauty Pentacle, allowing the flow of this energy to push through any blocks or obstacles that you may be feeling. Beauty, devotion, creativity, desire, expression. Continue to run the pentacle until you feel that you are back to neutral, having released anything unnecessary. (Pause.)

Now consider the beauty of the greater world around you. How do you feel about the wider world, both natural and human created? Do you feel connected to the world outside your home? Do you feel connected to the natural world? Sit with the idea of the world's beauty and see how this might show up in your body. Breathe through any tightness or difficulty. (Pause.)

Run the Beauty Pentacle, allowing the flow of this energy to push through any blocks or obstacles that you may be feeling. Beauty, devotion, creativity, desire, expression. Keep running this energy through your body until you feel back to neutral. (Pause.)

Consider now your inner beauty. Do you feel that you are a beautiful person? How do you know if someone is beautiful beyond external appearance? How much do you value a person's inner beauty? Contemplate these ideas and see how this might show up in your body. Breathe through any tightness or difficulty. (Pause.)

Run the Beauty Pentacle, allowing the flow of energy to clear out these thoughts and feelings. Let this energy clear out any obstacles or blocks. Beauty, devotion, creativity, desire, expression. Keep running the Beauty Pentacle until you feel yourself back to neutral. (Pause.)

Return your focus to your breathing. Focus on the gentle in-hale and exhale, and as you do, pull your edges back in. Allow your edges to firm up and return to normal. Breathe, letting everything else fall away except for your breath and body. When you feel ready, slowly open your eyes and pat your edges. Place your hands on the top of your head and say your name out loud three times.

Drink the glass of water that you left out for yourself and take time to write anything that came up during your contemplation.

COMMUNITY DEVELOPMENT

The following exercise should help you connect to the beauty of community. Can you step outside your space and see the beauty outside your door? When we can honor our communities, we enter into relationship with them. This relationship has the potential to heal ourselves and the world around us.

DISCOVERING BEAUTY
Beauty Walks

This piece of magick can be done at any time and any place, but I have found it to be the most effective when I have enough time to fully devote to the activity. Beauty walks will help you to see beauty in each step you take, no matter where you take them. I prefer to go to a wild natural place, but an urban environment works too; just make sure you can walk with as little talking as possible.

Start with breathing. Take a moment to focus on your breath and notice all of your parts and pieces. Notice if you are distracted or pulled somewhere other than the present moment. Pull on any threads that are leading you anywhere except the present moment. With each breath, draw any loose threads back into your body. Any place where you are stuck or feeling called in a different direction, just release that distraction and call that piece of yourself back to your body. Continue to do this until you feel full and present in the moment.

As the threads of you come back into your body, allow them to gather in your center. Perhaps this is in the center of your body. Perhaps this is at your navel. Perhaps this is right in the center of your pelvic bowl. Wherever center is for you, pull all of your awareness into it. Continue breathing as you shift your energy. Allow any distracting thoughts that awaken in your mind to just roll by, bringing your awareness back down into your center.

When you feel ready, begin your walk. Take notice of the beautiful things around you. The beauty you encounter may not be obvious. Notice the small things, the shadows, the weird, and the interesting. Do all of this with your awareness firmly seated in center. Anytime your awareness starts to creep back up or your mind chatter tries to distract you, stop your walk, breathe, and let your focus go back to your center.

Look for signs, omens, or messages that may come to you on this beauty walk. Pay attention to the environment that you're in. Look, listen, and be a part of that environment. You may want to stop along the way and write down anything important or interesting as it happens. You may want to pick a flower, a leaf, or a petal and press it into the pages of your book. You may want to take photos along the path. Or you may want to wait until you return to your starting point and remember the pieces as they come back to you. Let your walk unfold.

When you return to your starting point, take time to release your bundled-up awareness. Let your thoughts and energy return to their normal state. Make sure you give yourself the time and space to write down anything important or interesting from this experience.

Global Development

The following exercises should help you connect to the beauty of the world. How can you take beauty beyond your life? Can you hold your beauty on a personal level and still hold the beauty of the planet? When we remember that we are of the earth, how can we feel anything but beautiful?

Ritual: Opening Your Eye to Beauty

We all have an inherent eye for things that are beautiful. And what each of us finds beautiful is unique. But to delve into the power of the Beauty Pentacle, it is important to attune your seeing eyes, and your inner eyes, to the beauty in the world around us.

The following ritual should be done when you have an hour to dedicate to the process. In this ritual, as with all rituals in the book, allow it to unfold slowly. Don't rush to do the steps in order to check things off of your list. The work of the Beauty Pentacle is not a checklist. It is a gentle sigh, a sweet fragrance, a soft touch. It should be slow and lovely and lush. Giving yourself the space to explore beauty is, in and of itself, beautiful.

Supplies: A white candle of any size, a bunch of fragrant flowers, something soft (like a silk scarf, a chenille blanket, a piece of fur, or whatever else appeals to your sense of touch), something sweet to eat, soft music, and something soft and cozy to sit on.

Set Up: Set up your beauty altar with all of the supplies listed above in a way that is pleasing to your eyes.

Ritual: Begin by sitting in the comfortable place that you have prepared. Take a deep breath and feel your center. Give yourself
some time to fully arrive—mind, body, and spirit—into the
place you are currently inhabiting. When you feel fully present
and ready to begin, light the candle and start the music.

Take some time to listen to the music. How does it make you
feel? Where do you feel it? Let the music seep into you: breath,
blood, and bone. Hear the beauty of the music, the magick of the
music. Let the sound of beauty slowly expand your awareness.

When you feel ready, look at the bunch of flowers on your altar. Let your eyes feast on the colors, shapes, and textures of these
green bloods, these plants. Think about the magick and wonder
of plants growing. Smell the blossoms, taking in the sweetness of
each flower. Drink in the scent with your nose and let it fill you
up. How do these scents make you feel and where do you feel
them? Fill yourself up with the beauty of the flowers.

Again, when you feel ready, pick up the blanket, cloth, or fur
that you have placed on the altar. Run your fingers across it, taking in the tactile expression of this piece. Run that fabric across
your skin, over your arms, feet, neck, and face. How does this
make you feel? Soak up the beauty of this item through your
hands and skin.

Set down the fabric and pick up the sweet food. Smell the
sweetness. Look at the shape and size of this item. Feel its texture
with your fingers. And finally, bring this food to your lips, running it across your soft skin before biting into it and letting the
flavor of the sweetness caress your taste buds. Breathe in, allowing the fullness of flavor to consume you.

When all of your senses are swimming in beauty, take note of how this feels. Let this feeling expand around you, awakening your critical eye to the power of beauty. Look around the space that you are in, beyond the altar that you have created. Notice how your senses easily focus on the beauty around you. If possible, get up and move around the space. What else is beautiful? Where else can you find beauty? Take time to explore the beauty that is just within your reach. When you feel complete in the exploration, return to your seat at the altar.

Let beauty be a flame of power within you. Gather all of the beauty that you have been feeling and running through your body, and allow it to band together in your third eye—that spot between and above your normal seeing eyes. Let this beauty grow into a flame of power that burns brightly, connecting you to all of the beauty that is around you. Let that flame of power connect you to all of the beauty in the world, in every step you take. Let that flame settle, becoming a part of you that is constantly on alert.

Breathe, taking in how you might now feel different. Continue touching that flame throughout your day, allowing the beauty to fully integrate with your body and your third eye.

DISCOVERING BEAUTY
⟍ Google Earth ⟋

One of my role models is RuPaul Charles. I often refer to him (jokingly and seriously) as my "guru." (And I've been saying that for years, well before his book by the same name came out, thank you very much!) RuPaul may not be a Witch or a Pagan, but he sure does use language that makes me think we have more in common than might appear at first glance. In his book *GuRu,* he talks about how easily we can get stuck on small insignificant problems that keep us from seeing beauty in the world. RuPaul says, "Oh, I'm focused on this one small thing over here? The truth is, that's not that important."[22] It's like a reality check.

Life can be harrowing, stressful, difficult, sad, even ugly and traumatic. But that is not all of life. Even within the hardships we face there is still beauty, mystery, and magick. We can get so focused on the minutiae of what is going on in our own individual lives that we can lose sight of how awesome the world truly is.

In his book, RuPaul suggests going to Google Earth and looking up any place on the planet from a perspective where you can't see the specifics of the terrain.[23] Look at the perspective of where that place is in relation to where you are. Look at how massive the world truly is. Drill down on Google Earth, getting closer and closer. Use technology to examine the landscape, explore the street views, and look at this place in detail. Let the magick of the internet expand your awareness and let you sink into this place.

Remembering how small we are isn't meant to make us feel bad or insignificant, but rather, it is an opportunity to remember how big and beautiful the world truly is. There is so much potential, magick, and mystery that we are a part of. We are a part of the web of life on this planet. What is happening on the other side of the world still impacts us, but the weight of it is subtle and imperceptible. Remembering our place in that web can be a reality check and a step back into the beauty of the world.

---

22. RuPaul, *GuRu* (New York: Dey St., 2018), 158.

23. RuPaul, *GuRu*, 158.

Final Beauty Ritual

Once you have worked through all of the exercises and rituals in this section it is time to create a ritual for yourself to honor and acknowledge the beauty that you have created in your life. You will need a full day for this ritual. You may want to include others in the working to help share more of the beauty with the world.

Take time to plan your day in advance. The Beauty Ritual should be unique and individually created for you and how you look at beauty. This ritual is made up of four parts based on the elements, each incorporating beauty in your own personal way.

These ritual suggestions can be done in any order. Let your intuition and imagination lead this ritual. Follow your instincts. Do what appeals to you the most. Let yourself be immersed in beauty for one full day. This is a ritual to see the beauty around you, connect with your own beauty, and pamper yourself. At some point during your day, write a love letter to yourself and hold onto it for the longer ritual that should begin after dark.

Air
Listen to your favorite music
Sing
Play musical instruments
Spend time outside in the fresh air

Fire
Create a fire and scry into the flames
Dance
Visit a sauna or steam room
Get a Reiki treatment

Water
Go to a body of water
Swim
Soak in a tub
Drink your favorite drinks

Earth
Go to a park, grove of trees, or wild space
Adorn yourself in clothes that make you feel beautiful
Eat a meal of your favorite foods
Gather flowers, herbs, or foliage to decorate your altar

Spend the day doing a mixture and combination of these things. Plus, add several of your own ideas. Make the day as luscious and beautiful as possible. When you feel ready, go to your beauty altar and refresh it. This might require you to take it fully down, wipe down the surface, and then reassemble it. You may want to add new items to your altar that you gathered during the day, or you may feel called to take some things away. Take your time with this process. Sing or play music if you feel so called.

When your altar is set up, read your love letter out loud to yourself while looking into your beauty mirror. After you have finished reading your love letter, say to yourself, "You are beautiful." Sit in contemplation for as long as feels necessary. Look at yourself in the mirror. Do anything else that you feel called to do while in this space; take all the time that you need. This is a ritual of celebration of your beauty.

Once your contemplation is complete, enjoy a meal of your favorite foods or the foods that you only let yourself have on special occasions. Take time with each bite to savor the flavor and taste. Eat slowly, noticing the temperature and texture of the food. If you have been working with any godds or allies during this day, make sure to give them offerings of what you are eating.

✦ ✦ ✦ CHECK-IN ✦ ✦ ✦
HOW'S IT GOING?

Take out your journal. Read over the following questions and give yourself time to write down your thoughts. After working through the beauty point, how have your feelings on beauty changed? Do you find yourself noticing the beauty in the world more often? Look back over the challenges that you've faced and write what comes up for you when you see all that you have accomplished.

Chapter 6
Devotion

There is a large room thick with the smoke of spicy incense. The scent is heady and strong. Through the haze you can see hundreds of devotees kneeling before a massive painted statue of their godd. Each of the people in this room are chanting in a language that you cannot understand, but hearing it makes the hair on the back of your neck stand on end. The scene is of beautiful devotion.

An elderly couple holds hands as they stroll through the park on a hot summer's day. They stop midway down the walkway and kiss before shuffling along again, slower than the other people jogging or bustling from one place to another. They reach the edge of the park and one of them steps down off of the curb, extending a hand to their partner, helping them carefully and cautiously step into the street. The devotion they have for each other is palpable.

A woman sits on a wooden plank hundreds of feet up in the air, cradled in the arms of a massive redwood tree. She has been living this modest and dangerous life for close to two years, and this lifestyle will go on for much longer. She is exposed to the elements, scarcity, and her own loneliness, and yet she stays, understanding that the mission is more important than her discomfort. The years lived in the boughs of this tree have been done out of complete and utter devotion to the life of the tree and the spirit of the forest around her.

When you start to see, feel, and experience the beauty in the world, it awakens feelings of devotion. The power of the Beauty Pentacle flows from beauty to devotion because once you find yourself falling in love with the beauty of your neighborhood, or a tree, or a forest grove, or a house, or virtually anything, it awakens a passion to care for that thing—to devote yourself to it. Devotion awakens feelings of protection for the beauty in the world. When you recognize the beauty of something, you are more likely to devote some of your time and energy towards keeping it safe, clean, and healthy.

The energy center of devotion calls you to open your heart to the world around you. Now that you are starting to regularly tap into the beauty of the world, the next step is to give back to that space. The power of devotion asks for you to expose your vulnerability to that beauty, to feel it and connect with the world around you.

In the pentacle point of beauty, we practiced opening our eyes and senses to all that is beautiful. As we move to focus on the pentacle point of devotion, you are asked to take that beauty deeper, to feel it in your marrow and offer some of yourself to it in return. Devotion is the practice of honoring the beauty and giving back to it. Devotion calls us to deepen our connections to the things that we have found so beautiful. It is a giving back to the very concept of beauty—still a personal relationship.

The energy center of beauty resides in the top of your head. As the Goddess draws the power of beauty onto your physical form, her first line moves downward into your right foot. This is where devotion is activated. This is the power center of devotion in your body.

As this power is activated, you may find yourself facing some hard questions. Is there anything that you would devote your life to? Is there anything that you have already devoted your life to? Why? What in the world would you risk it all for? This isn't a romantic ideal. Seriously, ask yourself what would you give complete devotion to? Devotion carries with it a measure of sacrifice, but the power of the Beauty Pentacle would never ask you to give away everything.

Life is cyclic. You give and you take. There will be times that you are overjoyed with your wins, and there will be times that you are smashed by your losses. When we enter into a state of devotion, the cycles turn into a beautiful kaleidoscope of colors and potential. By connecting into the power of devotion, you begin to see beyond the cycle to the heart of the wheel that keeps us turning. At the core—at the center—of that cycle is beauty.

Figure 3: Devotion Sigil

Personal Development

The following exercises will open up the energy of devotion in your personal life. This section will help you explore where your devotion lies, what you truly are dedicated to, and what you might be blocked by in your power of devotion. How do you feel about being devoted to something? How can you become more devoted to your life?

✦ ✦ ✦ Check-in ✦ ✦ ✦
WHAT IS DEVOTION?

Take out your journal and consider the following questions. Is there anything in your life that you feel devoted to? Does the word devotion bring feelings of burden or feelings of liberation? Give yourself time and space to write about the word "devotion" and how you currently connect to it.

Discovering Devotion
☾ Modern Vision Quest ☽

Many indigenous communities use the practice of going on a vision quest to help them attain information, grow spiritually, or complete a rite of passage. Often these vision quests include the use of psychoactive substances or deprivation of necessities like food, water, and shelter. On a vision quest, participants are often alone, having to process and react to what they see and experience completely on their own. It is rare and only undertaken with the greatest of intention and preparation.

The vision quest we are undertaking for the Beauty Pentacle is in no way, shape, or form what is practiced in indigenous communities. Hence the term: *modern* vision quest.

The vision quests of indigenous communities are done through the wisdom of tribal lineage and with a deep cultural and familial understanding. In a modern vision quest you will seek out signs, symbols, and information while you are open as widely as possible to the subtle cues in the world around you. The modern vision quest can be done in an urban, suburban, or rural environment. But it is not the same as a quest done from tribal lines.

Ideally for this modern vision quest you will leave your home and go for a walk. The walk can last as long as you need it to. However, if this isn't possible for your body, you can sit in your yard, look out of a window, or travel to a beautiful place where you might be able to sit on a bench.

The first step is to set your intention for the quest. Once you have practice with this process you can set an intention for anything you need guidance with. The modern vision quest can help you in areas far beyond the Beauty Pentacle. For this specific quest, you should seek out information on the power of devotion. Set your intention to see, experience, and discover the importance of devotion in your life.

Before leaving, take some time to journal your thoughts, feelings, and goals for the quest you are about to take. Take your journal and camera with you, just in case you feel called to take pictures of what you discover. You might want to take food or water if you plan to be out for a long time. Remember, this isn't a quest of deprivation, but of devotion.

Step outside and take several deep breaths. Notice how it feels to breathe with intention. Our bodies happily breathe for us without us having to give it a single thought. Breath is what connects us to the greater world. Our planet has a finite amount of air, each breath you take has been breathed millions of times before by plants, animals, and the ancestors. The power of the entire planet can be connected to every breath you take.

After you feel connected to your breath and its rhythm, shift your awareness to the threads of attention that might be distracting you. Notice any places where you feel pulled in a different direction. Simply unhook those threads and reel them back into your body. Imagine that you have fishing lines hooked into other places that don't currently need your attention. Detach them and pull those threads back home to your body.

As the threads of your awareness come back, gather them up in a glowing ball in the center of your body. Draw down your awareness from your head, letting it sink into your belly. Gather all of your glowing beautiful threads of awareness into a ball right in your center.

This is not a normal resting place for your awareness. It may try to sneak back up into your head. You might find your normal sight resuming. This is all totally normal. When this happens just stop, breathe, and let your awareness sink back down into your belly.

Begin your walk. Simply place one foot in front of the other and begin moving forward. Don't follow a specific route, don't plot out where you will go next, just keep walking. Let your awareness *see*. Let your awareness lead you. As you move on your path, take note of what calls to you. Take note of anything that is interesting, alluring, odd, beautiful, strange, or compelling. You may want to write things down so you remember them, or you may want to take pictures to refer back to later.

Walk until you feel complete and then return home. Once you get back, look over the notes and pictures you took. Give yourself space to remember your experience and what has stuck with you.

Write down anything interesting or any common threads. Write how these words, thoughts, and images fuel your connection to devotion.

Discovering Devotion
⟨⟩ Clean Up ⟨⟩

Developing a strong devotional muscle will require you to look at your relationship with yourself and your surroundings. Do you honor yourself and your needs with a sense of devotion? One simple way to shift your devotional relationship with yourself is to take care of your living space. This may be ridiculously easy or frighteningly challenging depending on your current level of cleanliness. I'm not asking you to be perfect, spotless, or white glove clean, but it is easier to focus on the beauty around you when you feel comfortable and clear in your living space.

Whether you live in a huge house or a small room, cleaning up takes time and hard work. This isn't just about clutter or messes, but about the dust on the ancestor altar, the soap scum on the shower door, and the pet hair on the carpet. (Yes, I am describing my own house here.) When I finally take the time to clear off the altar, scrub the shower door, and vacuum, it feels so good!

For the process of devoting to yourself, take time to really deep clean your home. If this isn't physically possible for you, look into paying someone to clean your space. If that isn't financially possible for you, look into asking friends, family, or even social services for help. Once your space is clean, it is easier to keep it that way. When you feel proud of your living space it brings a level of beauty and comfort into your life.

Start this process and keep it going.

✦ ✦ ✦ CHECK-IN ✦ ✦ ✦
WHAT'S BEEN BEAUTIFUL?

Take out your journal and contemplate the following questions. Give yourself plenty of time to write your feelings. Now that you've had some time to step into the power of devotion, how does that shift or alter how you see beauty in the world? Take some time to write down what has been beautiful in this journey, what feels shifting or expanding in your life. What beauty have you seen recently? What's been beautiful?

Ritual: Becoming the Magpie

As a way to open your eyes to beauty even further and take that awareness deeper to a place of devotion, the following exercise connects you with an animal that understands that beauty is everywhere. Magpies are collectors of beauty. They see something interesting, shiny, fabulous, or curious and they seek it out, collect it, and bring it home. The world, to a magpie, is filled with an endless supply of beautiful wonders. We talk about people who are distracted by shiny things as magpies, almost as an insult. But magpies have it right. Magpies are devoted to beauty. This ritual will open up your own magpie eyes in order to help you gather more beauty in your world.

Supplies: Cleansing herbs to burn, your purple beauty candle, an athame, and your beauty mirror.

Set Up: This ritual should be done at your beauty altar. Set things up in a way that is appealing to you.

Ritual: Burn the cleansing herbs and prepare to step into ritual space. Collect yourself by focusing on your breath and feeling your center. Continue to pay attention to your breathing until you feel calm and collected, ready to do magick.

Pick up your athame and cast a circle around your beauty altar in your favorite way.

Set the athame down and call upon the points of the Beauty Pentacle. Chant the words *beauty, devotion, creativity, desire, expression* until you feel the power of the pentacle thrumming within you.

Call on the sacred magpie. Say this: *I call upon the sacred magpie that sees beauty all around itself. I call upon the power of that wise bird that sees the beautiful thing and wants to take it home. I call upon my own inner magpie to awaken and see the sparkling, shining, shimmering beauty that is all around me. Welcome, magpie.*

Sit at your beauty altar and contemplate the power of observation and how it connects to devotion. Let the silence help you to open your inner wings and awaken your inner magpie. Breathe into the power of this bird spirit.

When you feel ready, pick up your beauty mirror and look yourself in the eyes. Notice the sparkle and shine of your eye. Awaken the eye of the magpie as a soft voice in the background. The magpie eye isn't meant to take over your regular seeing eyes but to help your eyes see the things you might normally overlook. Awaken that curious eye that sees beauty everywhere it looks.

When the magpie eye is open, set down your mirror and explore your space. What do you notice with this eye activated that you didn't notice before? Look at your beauty altar. Do you still like the way it is laid out? Make any changes you feel called to shift.

After you have explored with your magpie eye open, pick up your athame and open the circle that you created in your space.

For the next week, hold on to your inner magpie. Keep that part of you awake and alert. When you see something beautiful, shiny, interesting, or distracting, pick it up and bring it home. Of course, only take things that are not someone else's property, ridiculously large, dangerous, or illegal to take. Magpies are smart, they know this, so listen to that inner magpie.

Place the items that you have collected on your beauty altar. Let it become like a game of Elvish Chess where you keep collecting objects and have to fit them all onto one space in a beautiful and appealing way. Elvish Chess is typically played with a group, where each person takes a turn adding items or adjusting the layout. You can make this a solo activity by placing your collected items and moving or arranging them until it is "done." When is it done? Only you can determine that. At some point your altar will get pretty full. When this happens, take all of your collected items outside, either in your own yard or another outdoor space, and make a shrine to beauty with the objects. Maybe you'll attract a magpie!

Discovering Devotion
Walking

Moving around, walking, and being outdoors comes up a lot when doing the work to connect with the devotion point and the power of the Beauty Pentacle as a whole. That's because part of the work of the Beauty Pentacle is to reconnect and remember the beauty of the world around you. It's beautiful out there. All you have to do is open your eyes, step outside, and see. The more that you see the beauty that is around you, right now, the more your sense of devotion will activate.

Go for a devotional walk. Take a walk for devotion, in devotion, with devotion. What would it be like to fully immerse yourself in the process of strolling, looking at the world around you, and connecting to what is happening in the moment? How would it feel to be devoted to the process of taking a walk? Would this transform or change the way that you feel about walking?

This isn't something that can be done on a treadmill—although you could do a devotional walk on a treadmill focusing on the devotion of having a healthy body. But rather than just mindlessly walking, it is an exercise in looking around you, noticing what is happening in your neighborhood, and immersing yourself in the landscape—taking in the beauty all around you. Try adding a devotional walk into your daily practice for the following week. Take time after each walk to write down your feelings.

DISCOVERING DEVOTION
Honey Cakes

The following recipe is for a traditional honey cake. These are ideal for leaving as offerings or sharing with other Witches. When you cook or bake, holding an intention of devotion shifts the cooking process from a mundane activity into a magickal one. Cooking is very intimate, and your feelings will be transmitted into your cooking whether you are conscious of it or not. When making honey cakes, keep your mind and heart focused on the energy of devotion and fill your baking with love. These cakes are very easy to make and can be eaten plain or with an icing drizzle.

Ingredients

2 ½ cups flour
4 eggs, beaten
1 ¼ cups sugar
1 cup honey
½ cup safflower oil
½ teaspoon baking soda
2 ½ teaspoons baking powder
1 teaspoon allspice
½ teaspoon ground cinnamon
⅛ teaspoon nutmeg
½ teaspoon ground ginger

Preheat the oven to 350° F. Grease a 9 x 13 baking pan. Combine all of the ingredients together in one large bowl. When everything is fully combined, pour the mixture into the baking pan. Bake for 45 minutes or until a toothpick inserted into the center comes out clean.

Optional Icing

2 cups confectioners' sugar
1 ¼ cups orange juice
1 tablespoon milk

Combine all ingredients and whisk until smooth. Pour over the top of the cake.

✦ ✦ ✦ CHECK-IN ✦ ✦ ✦
BEAUTIFUL STRANGER

Pull out your journal and complete the following sentences:

- I experience feelings of devotion when ...
- I am devoted to ...
- When I see another person in devotion, it makes me feel ...
- Devotion is ...
- I express devotion by ...
- Devotion feels like ...

If you are feeling exceptionally brave, consider posting your responses on social media and encouraging your friends to answer these questions too. There is vulnerability in devotion—see what your friends might share with you.

DISCOVERING DEVOTION
Pie Slices of Life

Where are you devoting your energy? What parts of your life are getting the most attention? Do you want it to be that way? We often don't have a true idea of where we are putting our energy. As the great Ferris Bueller once said, "Life moves pretty fast; if you don't stop and look around once in a while, you could miss it." [24] Make sure that you aren't just riding along, putting too much energy into things you don't want to be. Devotion requires awareness of your current circumstances.

---

24. *Ferris Bueller's Day Off*, directed by John Hughes (1986; Los Angeles, CA: Paramount Pictures).

Take out a piece of paper and draw a large circle in the middle of it. This is your life pie. Looks delicious, right? On another sheet of paper write the following words:

- Fun/Play/Adventure
- Work/Career
- Family
- Community
- Romance
- Relaxation
- Spiritual Pursuits
- Time Wasting/Other

You determine what falls under what category. For one person watching television might fall under relaxation, but for another it could be time wasting. This is not an exercise of judging, but of taking inventory. Remember, your most powerful tool is discernment. Look at these categories; how much time do you give to each of these pie slices on a monthly basis?

Draw in your pie slices, making them as large or as small as they might be based on how much time you spend on each category. If you're feeling inspired, you might color each pie slice based on how it makes you feel. How does the breakdown of your pie slices of life make you feel? Does it seem balanced? Are there areas that you would prefer to be bigger or smaller? What steps could you take right now to start to balance the pie slices in a way that would better fit how you'd like your pie of life to be split up?

DISCOVERING DEVOTION
Tell the Truth

In the book *The Four Agreements*, don Miguel Ruiz shares the four pieces of Toltec wisdom for living a full and healthy life.

To "be impeccable with your word" is the first agreement. "It is so important that with just this first agreement you will be able to transcend to the level of existence I call heaven on earth," he writes.[25] If you make an agreement, keep that agreement. Watch how you speak to yourself. And most importantly, watch how you speak to others.

Being impeccable with your word also means telling the truth. It sounds so easy; just tell the truth. But it is actually a big challenge. Watch how many times a day you tell lies. I'm not just talking about big whopping lies, but little insignificant lies too. A lie is a lie. Bending the truth is bending the truth. Intentionally omitting information is not being impeccable with your word.

Make it a practice to tell the truth all day long for at least one day out of the month. If you don't have something nice to say, don't say anything at all. Notice how hard or easy this process is. Write down your experiences in your beauty journal.

✦ ✦ ✦ CHECK-IN ✦ ✦ ✦
MY DEVOTION

In your journal, answer the following questions. When in my life have I been fully devoted to something? How did this devotion work for me? How did this devotion not work for me? Was I able to balance the rest of my life with my level of devotion? How might I fully devote myself to something while still holding the balance of the rest of the needs of my life?

---

25. don Miguel Ruiz, *The Four Agreements: A Practical Guide to Personal Freedom* (San Rafael: Amber-Allen Publishing, 1997), 26.

Discovering Devotion
꩜ Your Myth ꩜

An important step in activating your sense of devotion to yourself is to make yourself a hero in your own life. Write the story of your life as if you were writing a myth from antiquity. Give yourself a beautiful name, like a deity. Fill out your origin story and how you gained the powers that you possess. As the story unfolds, consider drawing images for the characters. Perhaps make yourself a comic book character? The process of creating your own personal myth could be the work of many months while your imagination engages with the process. Let yourself have fun with it. As you come close to the end of the myth, make sure you have the ending match where you would like your life to go. Make your myth-writing process become a spell that leads you into the future that you desire.

Discovering Devotion
꩜ Gratitude ꩜

Several years ago, I went through a period of depression and high anxiety. Nothing I tried helped in the slightest bit. All of my regular practices were either too hard to do during this challenging time or they made me feel like a failure for not being able to turn myself around. I was in a spiritual crisis and didn't know what to do.

My mom suggested starting a gratitude journal. I rolled my eyes at the twee suggestion. As if writing down a list of things I was grateful for was actually going to help anything. It felt like a "love and light fluffy bunny" suggestion. I needed real help, not white light. But I was so desperate for anything to help me that I implemented that practice along with seeing a therapist.

Every night before going to bed I would make a list of five things I was grateful for. Some nights this was an easy task and the five things would just roll off the tip of my pen. But at first, more often than not, I would really struggle to even think of *one* thing that made me feel grateful. So I broke it down to the simplest form and relied on one of my strongest gifts: snark.

Here is a real example of one of the entries from my gratitude journal:

Today I am grateful for:

- Drinking coffee
- Netflix
- Being able to read so I can pick a Netflix show
- Electricity so I can watch Netflix
- Distractions in the form of Netflix

As you can see, I was not always my best and brightest when making my lists. But there was something about the routine of it and the connecting into gratitude on a daily basis that helped me to see beauty. The more that I "had" to look for things to feel gratitude for, the easier it became for me to see good things as they were happening. This practice alone isn't what turned the tide on my anxiety, but it was one of the factors that gave me back some control.

As an act of devotion to yourself, start a gratitude practice. Before going to bed, write down at leave five things that you are grateful for. They can be big or small, silly or serious, but write them down. Let yourself feel grateful. When you need a boost, go back through and read your entries, letting them fill you with more gratitude.

DISCOVERING DEVOTION
☙ Prayer ❧

Prayer is a charged word. Witches and Pagans often connect prayer to religions other than our own. But no one faith owns prayer. One of the definitions of prayer is "an earnest hope or wish." Hope belongs to all of us and it has nothing to do with any specific deity or religion.

Of course, you can pray to a specific godd, and this can be done in devotion or in conversation. You can pray to the universe or the larger concept of a benevolent entity that we all return to. You can also pray to yourself, your higher self, your god-self.

Prayer is the release of your earnest hope or wish. It is a way to communicate the most important desire you are holding to a higher power. It is a way to ask for help, guidance, or both when it is needed most.

For the next week, start your day with a prayer. This can be done in any way that you feel called, but speak from the heart. Express your gratitude for what you have and ask for help, healing, and guidance for what you need. Call upon a godd, a higher power, or yourself to hear your prayers. Take notice of how this shifts your day and makes you more aware of the beauty around you.

INTERPERSONAL DEVELOPMENT

The following exercise will help your connection to devotion on an interpersonal level. This is not interpersonal with other humans, but rather, with a higher power. This section can show you where you might want to develop relationship with deity as a form of devotion and power. How do you connect to deity and trust in the relationship? How can you become more devoted to something other than your ego?

DISCOVERING DEVOTION
Devotion to Deity

Having relationship with deities is not a requirement to work with the energy of the Beauty Pentacle, but it can be another way to deepen the experience. Godds live in a reality that is just next to our own. Through the thinnest parts of the veils that separate us, we can have powerful relationships that fuel our spiritual work and help us grow in deep and profound ways.

You may already have godds that you are in relationship with. If so, incorporate your exercises with the Beauty Pentacle into the work that you already do with your deities. How does the energy of your deity shift how this work feels? Does your deity give you any additional insight or information about this energy?

If you don't currently have a relationship with a godd maybe now is the time to start one? There are a few godds listed in this book that are excellent to work with while processing the power of the Beauty Pentacle. You might start there. However, if you feel called, tapped, or interested in a specific deity, allow yourself to open up to the potential of a new relationship. Here are a few things you can do to start a new relationship with deity:

- Learn about them. The first step with any new relationship is to read their stories, myths, and tales.

- Learn about their cultures and the regions of the world where they originated from, both the ancient cultures and the modern ones.

- Create space for them. Set up an altar or devotional space where you can leave offerings or commune with them.

- Start communicating. Open up conversation and listen to what they have to say. Pay attention to signs and symbols that may pop up showing you that they are listening and willing to be in relationship with you.

Community Development

The following exercise will help you see the status of your devotion to community. Beyond what you are devoted to, how do you express that devotion? How do you honor your relationships with yourself, with your neighborhood, with the unseen? This section will help you refine your feelings of devotion and take action on sharing that with the world.

Discovering Devotion
Devotional Shrines

One of the ways we can show our devotion to someone or something is to build a shrine in its honor. There is no "right" way to build a shrine. A shrine is an expression of your devotion, so it should be aesthetically pleasing for you and your connection to the object of your devotion. A shrine should be a place where you spend time. Most importantly, a shrine is a place of devotion *to* something. Because of that, create a space that the object of your devotion would enjoy.

The first step is to determine what you want to build your shrine to. The second step is to just start building. Here are a few options on what you might want to create a shrine for:

Deity: Godds love to have shrines built for them. It is a great way to begin a relationship with a deity.

Nature Spirit: Perhaps there is a spirit in your home, neighborhood, or favorite wild place that you want to offer your devotion to.

Tree: There may be a specific tree or plant that you want to build a shrine for. Ideally this will be a tree that you have physical access to.

Large Area: You might consider building a shrine to your neighborhood, wild space, or town.

Ancestor: Ancestor shrines are found in cultures all over the world. Ideally an ancestor shrine will have photos or belongings of your ancestors.

After you have built the shrine, you are now responsible for that shrine. Take care of it. Leave offerings. Keep it clean. This is a place for you to express your devotion.

GLOBAL DEVELOPMENT

Being devoted to the planet and all its inhabitants may feel rather daunting. And that's true, it is a large task. However, it is our responsibility to take care of this planet. We can take many small steps every day that add up to big changes. We can help and tend our local environs, and that will reverberate across the planet too. The following exercises will show you simple ways to devote to the globe.

DISCOVERING DEVOTION
Healing the World
with Simple Acts

We humans could transform the world if only we could all agree on what the best transformation would look like. If only we could remember our connection to each other and to the land. There are millions of acts of valor happening all over the world right this moment. There are so many more healing, sharing, and positive acts happening than destructive or ugly acts. Imagine if we could gather up all of those good acts into a single massive energetic ball and use it, as if it was a healing balm, to heal the world.

The following trance can be done at any time. Ideally you will have thirty to forty-five minutes to complete the process without being disturbed. You will need a place where you can sit or lie down the entire time. It is best if you can record the following trance ahead of time and play it back.

Trance: Sit or lie down and get comfortable. Breathe deeply and slowly, allowing yourself to relax. Let your awareness begin to open up, spreading wider than your body. With each breath your awareness gets larger and larger, expanding beyond the room you are in.

Take a moment to think on all the other beings on the planet—every single person in every town, city, state, and country. Let your awareness spread wide and far, taking in the massive amounts of people that are all over the planet. (Pause.)

Let your awareness expand even larger. Let yourself become aware of all of the beings that have ever lived on this planet, going back to the beginning of time. Imagine all of the wealthy people, poor people, famous people, infamous people, kings, farmers, and all of the people that have ever existed through all of time. (Pause.)

Feel the massive amount of people and energy that has existed on this planet. Consider that each of these people, each of these lives, did at least one good thing at some point in their existence. Many of these lives did many wonderful, kind, and caring things. Many of these lives did amazingly positive things, changing the course of the world for the better.

Let your awareness take note of all of these positive acts. Imagine what could happen if you were to gather them all together. In your mind's eye begin to gather up all of these shimmering, shining positive acts. Use a broom and sweep them all together. Use your hands to catch any glowing pieces of positivity that may have fallen away. There are millions—billions—of good deeds to gather, each one of them glowing brightly.

Continue to gather these pieces into one bright, shining, and shimmering orb. This ball of energy condenses into a tight, compact glowing ball of healing. It is small enough that you can hold it in your hand.

Now visualize the entire planet swirling right in front of you—the whole of planet Earth. Set this healing ball of good deeds on the planet and watch as the glow melts into the Earth. All of the healing power, every positive act that you have gathered up, all of the good deeds, all of the kindness, all of the caring, is melting into the fabric of the planet. The glowing brings with it healing and balance. The planet now glows with peace, love, and caring. (Pause.)

Release this vision and switch your focus back to your body and to your breathing. Take note of the edges of your body and how you feel in this moment. Let yourself become aware of your surroundings and the current time and place where you reside.

When you feel ready, pat your edges, say your name out loud three times, and slowly open your eyes.

This trance can be done over and over again. The more often it is done, the more healing that is offered to the planet.

Ritual: Humble Yourself in the Arms of the Wild

Humbling yourself in the arms of the wild requires you to recognize your level of importance to the wild and greater world around you. This is not to say that you aren't important. You are! However, humans have fallen into the misguided—and so wrong—belief that we are *the most* important creatures on the planet. This is simply not true. We are part of the fabric that is the tapestry of this world, but no one thread is more important than another. As an act of devotion, complete the following exercise to express that devotion to the world.

The following ritual can be done with a group or as a solitary. It requires being outdoors. The wilder the place, the better, but as Witches we work with what we've got, so use the wildest space you have access to. This ritual requires no set up or supplies other than yourself, a wild space, and your journal.

When you reach your wild space, take a moment to center yourself. Look around the space you're in. Really look. Notice the color of the leaves, the smell of the grass, the shape of the landscape. Breathe deeply of this place and let it connect with you. Take some time to notice how you feel in this place. Do you feel a part of it or like an intruder?

Get down on the ground. Yes, this might be hard. It might be uncomfortable. Yes, this might be impossible. Get as much of your skin on the ground as you possibly can. If this ends up only being the bottoms of your feet, that's great. If it's possible for your body, completely lie down on the ground, face down if you can.

Breathe. Breathe in rhythm with the earth below you. Feel your connection to the soil, the sand, the dirt, the roots, the loam, the needles, the *ground*. How does this connection feel?

Does this feel easy? How do you connect with the earth below you? Is this a smooth or challenging connection to make?

Humble yourself. Speak to the earth. Tell the earth how much you love her. Tell the ground why you appreciate it. Express your gratitude for the wildness that runs through your veins. Speak from the heart and allow the words to come as they need to. Speak these words into the earth, let the vibrations of the words flow from your mouth into the ground. Let her feel those vibrations.

Allow this process to unfold as it wants to. When you feel ready, thank the earth, the ground, for holding you. Slowly and carefully get back up and take some time to journal anything important or interesting that came up during your time.

FINAL DEVOTION RITUAL

Before starting this ritual, you will need to decide what it is you are going to devote yourself to. Perhaps it's a godd or a spirit; perhaps it's your own heart or your home. Maybe it's work, a pet, or a plant. It doesn't matter what you choose but choose something.

Keep in mind that through this ritual you are opening up to a devotional relationship to something else. This should not be taken lightly. Give plenty of time and space to deciding what you will give yourself over to. Be ready to honor the commitment after the ritual is complete.

Supplies: Gather supplies for an altar. This is not your beauty altar, but rather a new creation that represents your devotion. Choose items that are beautiful, appealing, and connect to the spirit of devotion for your chosen entity. Arrange to play music that is both appealing to you and connects to the spirit of your devotional act. Get incense, food, and drink that all connect to your devotional act.

Set Up: Use all of your supplies to create an atmosphere that connects you to the spirit of your devotion. Set up a place for food and drink, play your music, light your incense, and prepare to set up your devotional space.

Ritual: Once your space is set up, take a moment to ground and center yourself. Stand with your feet firmly planted on the ground and feel your connection to the world around you. Breathe deeply, connecting to the gift of air as it enters and exits your body. Feel the center of your body and continue breathing until you feel calm, collected, and ready.

Run the Beauty Pentacle through your body. Run the points: *beauty, devotion, creativity, desire, expression.* Start slowly, letting the power of the pentacle build. Let the flow of the energy move faster and faster until it is thrumming through your body. Breathe in the power of the pentacle.

Listen to the music playing and let it connect you to your devotion. Take in the scent of the incense, look at the items you have collected to create your altar. Let all of these things awaken the power of devotion within you. Feel that energy in your heart, hands, gut, and head. Devotion.

Speak out loud of your devotion. Express this devotion with your own words from the heart. Call to the spirit of your devotion, letting that spirit know why you choose to devote to it and how you will honor that commitment. Let the words flow out of you, trusting what comes without it having to be perfect.

When you feel ready and you've said all of the words that need to be said, begin setting up the altar space. Use your intuition and listen for any messages from the subject of your devotion. Let this unfold slowly, trusting in the process as you go. The last step of setting up this place of devotion is to leave offerings. Set out food and drink or whatever else feels appropriate for your devotion.

Take time to write down any messages that you might have received during your ritual. Clean up the ritual space and move forward in your life with awareness of this new commitment that you have taken on.

Much like a spiritual initiation or a marriage ritual, a devotional ritual changes us in ways that may be obvious or imperceptible. Over the next few days, notice how you feel and any changes that may be coming about due to this new commitment that you have undertaken.

✦ ✦ ✦ CHECK-IN ✦ ✦ ✦
HOW'S IT GOING?

Take out your journal and consider the following questions. After working through the devotion pentacle point, how have your feelings on devotion changed? Do you find yourself noticing beauty in the world around you more often? Look back over the challenges that you've faced and write what comes up for you when you see all that you have accomplished.

CHAPTER 7
CREATIVITY

A young artist stands in front of a paint-splattered canvas. Her arms and fingers are covered in splotches of color. The wooden tip of her brush is pressed against her lip as her eyes scan the canvas for the next step. She hums softly, unaware, immersed in the process of developing her piece. A small smile creases the corners of her mouth as her hand fervently returns to applying paint on the scene she is building.

His big strong hands press into the dough. He pushes the pad of his hand through the mixture over and over again. The dough is gathered into a ball and flung down on the table as he has done thousands of times before. This bread is for his family. This bread will feed them for many days. It is made with a recipe that he has developed over many trials and errors. He loves this part of the baking process and kneads that love into the dough as he shapes it.

Her trembling hands hold the flute up to her lips. It has been years since she's played, and she isn't really sure that she remembers how to anymore. She exhales, focusing her breath across the mouth of the instrument. A shaking, wavering note escapes. She wiggles her fingers across the keys, making a cacophony of noise, and smiles; a whisper of something awakens. A faint thread of memory flutters by and she grasps onto a string of notes. Her fingers follow the old and long-forgotten memory. One simple song is all she remembers, but it is enough to spark her creativity and the music she once loved so much.

Beauty and devotion awaken creativity. When we are able to see beauty, finding it in all the places we look, we will find a strong pull towards devoting ourselves to that beauty. What better way to devote to beauty than to create more beauty? An offering. A song. A day picking up trash. Creativity takes on many shapes and forms, but its source flows from the power of beauty.

However, creativity is not easy. In fact, creativity is immensely challenging. Our culture puts a lot of pressure on creativity. Many of us hold this notion that in order to be creative we have to live up to some external standard. Our creativity must be good enough based on the judgment of sources outside of ourselves. We may feel that our creativity doesn't count if it doesn't earn an income, become a side hustle, get exploited on social media, or be recognized by others.

Creativity isn't something that only the elite or classically trained possess. All humans are creative. The shape, color, sound, and experience of that creativity will be different for each person. Our creative voice might have always been a roaring noise that we can easily hear and honor, but just as likely, it may be a small voice that is timid, shy, and quiet. Exploring that voice and making space for it to communicate with us is vital to the energy of the Beauty Pentacle.

The power of beauty flows from the top of our heads, down our bodies, and into our right foot. As the Goddess continues to draw on us, she moves from our right foot to our left hand, coming to rest at that energy center—the place of creativity.

The act of being creative is an act of beauty. It doesn't matter if you have an art form that you already know and love or if art seems like something a million miles away from your reality. All humans are creative. And creativity doesn't have to involve art.

I once had a mentor ask me if I was wasting my creative energy on finding ways to not be creative. Of course, this was true. Creative energy can be put to use in ways that don't serve you. Creativity can be wasted living in fantasy worlds, movies, television, and video games. It can be squandered on work that dulls your senses and bores your mind. It can be turned into busywork preventing you from digging into the beauty all around you.

Creativity doesn't have to be for anyone but you. In fact, creativity is best when it is done only for you without worry or direction from anyone else. This doesn't mean that you shouldn't take lessons, find a teacher, or study from masters if your heart calls you to do so. But develop your creative skills for the love of being creative. Hone your skills for the joy of it. Let your happiness, joy, fear, frustration, pain, story, and beauty all flow through your creative endeavors.

Many people confuse the idea of creativity with expression, which is the last point of the pentacle. Let me be clear on the difference. Expression isn't necessarily creative and not all creativity gets expressed. In the tool of the Beauty Pentacle, creativity is a power just for you. It doesn't need to be given away. It doesn't need to be shared. It is only a voice that needs to be listened to.

On the other hand, expression is the sharing of that creativity. Expression is the pouring out of the energy that you have built up, the saying what needs to be said. The difference between these two points may seem subtle, but once you start working through their energy the differences will become more profound.

Figure 4: Creativity Sigil

PERSONAL DEVELOPMENT

The following exercises are designed to spark creativity in your life. This section should power up the energy center of creativity within you. You may discover personal blocks or obstacles through these exercises; work through them and don't give up. Through the personal development section your creativity will be sharpened and honored. How can you open up to creativity?

✦ ✦ ✦ CHECK-IN ✦ ✦ ✦
WHAT IS CREATIVITY?

Get out your journal and write on the topic of creativity. This might seem like a simple and obvious answer. Perhaps creativity equals art? Perhaps creativity equals creation? Perhaps it is something else altogether? What about when creativity is used negatively? What about the times you are creative in avoiding what needs to be done? What about the ways you are creative in not dealing with "the thing"? How does creativity show up in your life? How much space do you make for it? And does it feel like an important part of who you are? How and why?

DISCOVERING CREATIVITY
Intention Map Book

A piece of magick that I have done for well over two decades is the practice of making an intention map. For many years I did these on my birthday as a way of creating a visual spell for what I wanted to draw into my life in the coming year. This would serve as a touchstone for me, and often it would help me to see how I was truly manifesting my desires in ways other than my logical mind expected me to.

I've heard intention maps also referred to as spell collages, intention charts, intention collages, spirit boards, intention boards, and even art spells. Creating an intention map starts with a large blank piece of paper and a stack of old magazines. You go through the magazines, cutting out any words or images that strike a positive reaction in you. Cut out anything beautiful, powerful, or in alignment with what you want to manifest in your life.

Once you have all the images and words cut out, you arrange them on your piece of paper in a collage that is pleasing to your eyes.

In this specific working, I invite you to take the intention map one step further. Instead of one big sheet of paper, get a large journal with blank pages. Perhaps this journal could be your Beauty Pentacle Book of Shadows, or another book altogether. Inside these pages affix beautiful images, poetry, words, phrases, and art that appeals to your beauty eye. Also within these pages press flowers, save seeds, put in a lock of your lover's hair, and anything else that strikes your fancy. Write down your spells, put in clippings of photographs, and affix feathers you've collected (with awareness that not all feathers are legal to possess). Let this be a beautiful collection of magick.

Another option besides a blank journal is to get a big old used book and do the same thing. The bonus of a big used book is the ability to include the words from the book. You can cut out pieces, cross out words, black out sentences, and use what is already there to incorporate your own beauty into an old and forgotten book.

Whether you start with a blank paged journal or an old book, let this book become an intention map of beauty. When you open the pages you should feel inspired by the beauty that you've created within them.

Discovering Creativity
Bibliomancy

Divination goes hand in hand with the Beauty Pentacle. Divination requires a keen connection to beauty and an awakened intuition.

While doing the work of the Beauty Pentacle and running beauty energy through your body, you may have already discovered blocks or obstacles. One way to get information on areas where you feel challenged is with divination, specifically bibliomancy.

Bibliomancy is the art of using the written word to reveal insight into a situation. This connects to creativity because all books, no matter the form or style, are an expression of creative energy. Using bibliomancy in connection to your creative self is the perfect form of divination.

Bibliomancy can also open your creative mind. The answers that you receive may be a little like the answers given by the oracle at Delphi, a bit of a riddle. It may require your creative self to dissect the message and grasp its true meaning for you.

When you find that you have a question that requires some outside guidance, pull out a book—the bigger and thicker the better. I prefer to use poetry books or spiritual books, but any book will do. State your question or issue out loud and then flip through the pages of the book.

When you feel called, stop flipping the pages and allow the book to fall open. Without looking at the words, slide your finger along the page until you notice an urge to stop. When this happens, look down at the words where your finger stopped and read the sentence you have landed on.

Let this sentence inform the area where you need guidance or information. Keep track of any revelations in your journal.

DISCOVERING CREATIVITY
⟡ Tarot Mandala ⟡

Creating something beautiful is all part of this work. You don't need any fancy art supplies or training to make a spectacular art piece. *Mandala* is the Sanskrit word for circle. The mandala is used in many Eastern philosophies as a meditation or creative practice for esoteric concepts. A mandala in Buddhist practice is meant to be temporary. Monks will spend hours—sometimes days—creating an intricate art piece only to sweep it up once complete.

The following exercise follows the same concept as a mandala, but rather than using paint, colored sand, or paper and pencils, you will use tarot or oracle cards.

This piece is best done with a group of people. Invite as many friends over as you feel comfortable sharing this work with. Ask each person to bring a deck of tarot or oracle cards. Sit in a circle and focus on beauty. Give space for each participant to go through their decks of cards and pull out three to five cards that bring up feelings of beauty. Once everyone has their cards, lay them out in the center of the room, creating a mandala, or sacred design, for beauty.

Take your time to look at the beauty that has been created together. Take note of similarities and differences. Look at how the colors, sizes, and shapes create a picture of beauty. Consider taking a picture of your beauty mandala. Take some time to discuss the mandala with the group. What do other folks notice? When ready, pick up the cards and return them to their original decks.

Follow this same process for all the other points: *devotion, creativity, desire,* and *expression.*

✦ ✦ ✦ CHECK-IN ✦ ✦ ✦
BEAUTIFUL STRANGER

Pull out your journal and complete the following sentences:

- The word "creativity" makes me feel ...
- I am creative when ...
- I enjoy being creative when ...
- Creativity is ...
- I express my creativity by ...
- Creativity feels like ...

If you are feeling exceptionally brave, consider posting your responses on social media and encouraging your friends to answer too. The more that we share beauty with others and engage in these conversations, the more the doors to beauty are opened and our eyes are uncovered.

DISCOVERING CREATIVITY
Letter to the Past

Every single person on the planet has had someone tell them they couldn't do something creative. Every single person on the planet has attempted something creative and been shut down, told it's not good enough, or laughed at. It doesn't matter how, when, or why this shutdown happened. What matters is getting back on the horse and creating something again.

When I was in the fifth grade, I joined the music group at my elementary school. There were only three of us in the group, all girls, all playing the flute. Our music teacher was a rather cranky old guy. He was the music teacher for our entire school district. I wasn't a very good flute player. I didn't practice as much as I should have. I got bored with it easily, but I did like music class.

One of the other girls was very good. I don't know if she was just musically talented or if she practiced a lot, but she was much better than I was. The third girl was somewhere in the middle. Not as terrible as I was but not as good as our "first chair" player.

I have a clear memory of one of our lessons. Our music teacher was exceptionally annoyed with our lack of skill. He told me that I would never make it into the high school band. No matter how hard I practiced I would never be good enough. Being the stubborn Taurus I am, rather than discourage me, it actually made me mad enough to want to prove his ass wrong.

By the time we got to junior high school, only two of the three of us were still playing the flute. I was still terrible, typically the last or second-to-last chair out of ten flute players. But I kept going with it. In fact, I loved being a part of the concert band, even if I was terrible.

By the time we got to high school, I was the only one left still playing the flute. Still terrible, that never changed, but I made it to the high school band. I didn't stop my creative outlet of playing music, because I did love it, just not enough to practice on a daily basis.

If I had let that old cranky man dictate my future experience, I never would have been a part of the high school concert band, which was a highlight of my teen years. It could have been very easy for me to hide, quit, or stop playing altogether.

Think back on a time when your creative self was admonished for not being good enough. Think back on a time when your creative self was crushed by the feedback from a mentor, teacher, parent, or idol. If you could go back in time and talk to that younger self, what would you tell them to encourage them to keep going in their creative endeavors?

Pull out your journal and write a letter to your past self who was told their creative expression wasn't good enough. Tell that shining being why they should not give up. Explain how important that creative outlet is. Encourage them to keep going.

Write this letter and then set it aside for at least a week. Try not to think about it. Although, keep in mind, when you start poking into memories like this, you are likely to have other memories and feelings pop up. After a week, pull this letter back out. Light a candle, burn some incense you love, and read the letter out loud.

Notice anything that comes up for you when reading this letter. Imagine your younger self sitting across from you, listening to this letter. See their—your—eyes light up with encouragement. See what it might have felt like to have been told that your creativity was a beautiful blessing. How would you feel now if you had been given encouragement then?

When done reading the letter, go and do something creative. Sing, dance, drum, draw, paint, mold, play the flute! Do whatever your creative self calls for. Be brilliant, be terrible, be silly, but be creative.

DISCOVERING CREATIVITY
⟡ Imagined Other Lives ⟡

There are many roads that we don't take. Maybe life forces us in a different direction. Maybe we choose the left path instead of the right. Life is full of choices. In making a choice, we don't

choose something else—for good or for bad. Setting aside a potential path can be hard, but we don't have to totally let go of
those lost paths.

I left college as a sophomore. At the time, I had a great corporate job. I was being promoted quickly, making more than
double that of my peers. It was easy for me to see where my life
was headed in the corporate world. I figured college was unnecessary. That worked well for me for many years, but the world has
changed a lot since 1999. Not having a degree has made it next to
impossible to even get a corporate job interview. What if I had
finished college? What if I had completed that degree? What
would my life look like now?

Set a space for yourself with a candle, your journal, and something to drink. Sit down and light the candle. Ask your guides
and allies to be present as you step into this working. Take a deep
breath and center yourself.

In your journal, make a list of five paths you didn't take. Have
a few of your five imagined lives be real options you could have
taken, like finishing college. But also let a couple of them be ri-
diculous fantasies that were never really possible. Like randomly
meeting Jason Priestley at a 7-Eleven in Los Angeles, falling
immediately in love, and running off together. (Okay, so that
might be one of my fantasies.) Have a couple of your imagined
lives just be silly and playful.

Make space to "time-walk," following the roads through these
imagined lives. What if you had followed that other path? What
chain reactions would be different than the life you are living
now? Write out the story of these five lives if you had taken those
paths and not the path you have been on.

Write these imagined lives out as if you are watching a story
unfold in front of you. If need be, give yourself a couple of jour-

naling sessions to finish up this process. Once you are finished, read back over your imagined lives. Are there any similarities? Are there any roads where there is overlap? Are there places in these lives where you feel a longing to go back? Are there things you want to incorporate into your life now?

Look at the places where you feel a longing. How can you make changes or adjustments in your life right now in order to start bringing these roads into your current path? What can you do in this life to create some of those imagined lives in your reality? Tomorrow take one step to pull that closer to you.

DISCOVERING CREATIVITY
෧ Release Shame ෨

Being creative will bring about dips into beauty, pain, hardship, and celebration. Opening up to your creativity may even bring you into the depths of fear. You may find doors that you have been working hard to keep closed rattling and shaking, the skeletons inside demanding attention.

We all carry around some form of shame, guilt, or sadness about something from the past. Artistic and creative endeavors give us a way to express these challenging feelings and make something awesome, beautiful, or transformative from it.

I drew a picture of my mom once when I was about eight. I had been watching a television show on PBS that taught you how to draw and thought I really knew what I was doing. My mom was less than impressed with my drawing and in a less-than-stellar mom moment reacted with, "Do you think my nose looks like that?!" when I showed her my artwork.

Over thirty years later, I get how a tired and overworked mom, with some sensitive feelings about her nose, might make that statement. But as an eight-year-old budding artist, I was pretty crushed. I didn't get that she was projecting her self-conscious feelings onto my drawing, I just thought I sucked. I stopped drawing after that.

We all have stories like this too. There is some shame around this story for me, shame around my relationship with my mother, and shame about not being good enough. The not-good-enough shame has been an ongoing issue my entire life. It shows up in lots of places and relationships. It is one of my shadows. And so I have to work on it and with it.

Write a list of where you feel shame. Take this letter outside and carefully burn it in a fireproof container. Burn the paper down until there is nothing but ash. Then release the ashes to the winds. Watch as your shame floats away, no longer yours; release it.

Take a moment to cleanse after releasing the ashes. Choose your favorite method. Smudge or sain yourself with burning herbs, take a cleansing bath, spray yourself with a smokeless incense, whichever method you like best.

Return to your writing and make a list of the things that you are proud of. Write down all of the things that you have accomplished, the big things and the little things. When you are finished with the list, go back outside and read the list to the winds. Let your voice carry what you've accomplished out into the world. Keep this list and refer to it any time you need a boost.

DISCOVERING CREATIVITY
⸙ Take a Break ⸙

Give yourself time away from this work. Take a solid week off of reading, journaling, contemplation, or running the pentacle. See how it feels to set the practice down for a few days. If possible, simplify all of your other spiritual practices too. Give yourself a break from self-improvement. Ultimately it will be good for you.

After a week, pick the pentacle work back up. Start writing in your journal again. Bring your spiritual practices back into your daily activities. How does it feel to shift back into these practices? Is it easy and smooth or rough and challenging?

DISCOVERING CREATIVITY
৩৩ Inspiration Date ৩৩

In order to awaken to the power of the Beauty Pentacle and the energy center of creativity, commit to taking yourself on an inspiration date at least once a week. This might feel like a challenging commitment, but it is an important one. It is a step to prove your dedication to yourself, your creativity, and the beauty of the world.

On an inspiration date go somewhere beautiful. Go to an art gallery, take a walk through a park, attend a play, go to a concert, explore a place you've never been before. Get out and do something that fills you up with beauty.

While out and about, take photos, pick up business cards or brochures, and pick flowers and put these into your journal. Keep track of anything odd, interesting, or joyful that happens while on your date.

DISCOVERING CREATIVITY
৩৩ Trance to Meet Your Creativity ৩৩

When you work with an energy center enough it can start to take on a life of its own. With the creativity point, the more you are creative, the stronger this energy becomes. It then becomes possible to commune with this energy. By having a strong relationship with your creativity, you can garner a lot of information you would otherwise be without.

This exercise should be done when you have thirty to forty-five minutes to devote to the process. If you can do this trance with other folks, great! Have one of the people read the trance. If not, record yourself reading it and play it back when you are ready.

Find a place where you can sit or lay down undisturbed. Make sure that you are comfortable and make any adjustments to keep it that way throughout the trance. Have your journal and a glass of water handy for after the trance.

Trance: Take a deep breath. Feel the expansion of your lungs. Breathe with intention—in and out. Notice how a long, slow breath helps your body to calm, relax, and slow down. Keep breathing noticing the inhale and exhale. (Pause.)

Notice your edges, the edges of your body, and how it feels to be you in this time and place. Let your awareness sink down to the tips of your toes. Visualize your toes surrounded by a warm, bright light. Every piece of you that this light touches is left relaxed and calm. As you breathe, each of your toes is touched by this light.

The warm light moves upward, wrapping around your ankles. And it moves further upward, covering your shins and calves in a warm, relaxing glow of light. The light covers your knees and thighs, leaving every bit of you relaxed and warm. (Pause.)

This light continues to move upward, surrounding your pelvic bowl, your belly, and your lower back, leaving you relaxed. The light moves up your rib cage and up your spine. This warm light swirls around your hips and sides. The glow covers your shoulders, moving down your arms, elbows, and hands. The light swirls around each of your fingers, leaving you relaxed and warm.

Again, the light moves up, swirling around your throat and neck. The warm glow covers the back of your head, your jaw, your cheeks, your temples, and around your eyes. The light swirls around your head, coming to a close at the top of your head. Now your whole body is covered in a warm glow—warm, safe, and relaxed.

From this place of relaxation, open your inner eye, that Witch's eye that sits right above and between your normal seeing eyes. Open that Witch's eye and see in front of you a path. Step forward onto the path, placing one foot in front of the other, continuing to move along. As you walk, take notice of what kind of landscape you are in and anything interesting in your sight. (Pause.)

Continue to move forward along the path, step by step, moving further and further with one foot in front of the other. Ahead of you, you notice a building. This place is the house of your creativity. Allow it to take shape as your steps continue to bring you closer to it. With each step forward, you can see more and more of your house of creativity more clearly. Allow this place to fully form, taking note of its size, shape, and style. (Pause.)

As you step up to your house of creativity, the door opens and you step inside. Take a look around this place. How is it decorated or furnished? Are there supplies for creativity accessible to you? Explore this space. (Long pause.)

There is a closed door in this place. You go to it and knock three times. The door opens and you step inside the room. Awaiting you is your creativity. What does your creativity look like? What is its size, shape, color, and expression? If it hasn't already, your creativity morphs into a human form. Take time to speak with your creativity. Ask the questions that you have been holding about your relationship with your creativity. Hear what it has to say. (Pause.)

Although you can visit your house of creativity at any time, your time here is limited for now. Say anything else that needs to be said before you leave this place. (Pause.)

Walk back out of the room and leave your house of creativity. Step back onto the path that brought you here, following it back the way you came. Again, take note of your surroundings and the landscape that is on either side of your path. Keep walking, shifting your awareness to follow the path, and step back into your body.

Allow yourself to become aware of your breathing. Shift your awareness, beginning to close your inner eye. Notice the edges of your body and how it feels to be in this time and this place. Close your Witch's eye and slowly open your normal seeing eyes.

Take some time to write down anything odd, important, or interesting from your experience. Drink the glass of water and slowly let yourself move back into the world.

DISCOVERING CREATIVITY
✦ Traveling Beauty Mirror ✦

The beauty mirror is the primary magickal tool of the Beauty Pentacle. But carrying around a large mirror for magickal work away from your beauty altar isn't practical. Having a traveling beauty mirror will give you the opportunity to do magickal workings with your mirror out in the world.

Get a small compact mirror. Of course you can find a compact mirror at a pharmacy, dollar store, or big-box store, but for this mirror take your time and find something exceptionally beautiful. Find an old antique compact or silver cigarette case that shines like a mirror when properly polished. Find a gorgeous old family heirloom that is hiding in a box in the garage. Find a small, artfully decorated box that you can affix a mirror to the inside of. Take your time and find the perfect little thing to serve as your traveling mirror.

Follow the beauty mirror ritual from the first section to bless and consecrate this small mirror.

Carry this mirror with you as often as possible. If you can keep it in a bag, purse, or pocket even better. The traveling beauty mirror should be used to "catch" beautiful moments. When you see a magnificent sunset, pull out your traveling beauty mirror and look at the scene through the reflection of the mirror. If you witness something fantastic, look at it through the reflection in the mirror.

Each time you use your mirror to capture the reflection of a beautiful or inspiring moment, the power of your traveling beauty mirror increases.

This is a two-way process. The more you charge the mirror by catching beautiful reflections, the stronger it gets, and then you can turn that around and use that energy to boost your own feelings around *beauty, devotion, creativity, desire,* or *expression.* When you need a personal boost of beauty, or anytime you aren't feeling yourself, look at your own reflection in the traveling beauty mirror. If you have a friend or loved one that is in a challenging place or feeling depleted, have them look at themselves in your traveling beauty mirror as a way to share your beautiful power with them.

> ✦ ✦ ✦ CHECK-IN ✦ ✦ ✦
> ## WHAT'S BEEN BEAUTIFUL?
> Pull out your journal and consider the following questions. Now that you've had some time to step into the power of creativity, how does that shift or alter how you see beauty in the world? Take some time to write down what has been beautiful on this journey, what feels shifting or expanding in your life. What beauty have you seen recently? What's been beautiful?

DISCOVERING CREATIVITY
Curiosity

A curious mind is one that will discover beauty wherever it goes. When you are curious, you will find yourself with the desire to explore, uncover, and discover the wild and beautiful things in the world. Some of us are naturally curious. A naturally curious person will crawl under an arched bush to see where it leads. A naturally curious person will try a new restaurant and eat something they've never tasted before. A naturally curious person will drive down a road they've never been on just to figure out where it might end up. A naturally curious person is always asking, "Why?"

Curiosity will bring more opportunities to find unexpected beauty because you are more likely to end up in an unexpected place.

For this working you will need to be undisturbed for thirty minutes in a place where you can sit or lie down comfortably. You will only need a journal.

Trance: Take a few deep breaths and allow yourself to sink into the place where you sit. Give yourself some space to just breathe.

Notice each inhale and exhale, letting your breath cleanse and open your awareness.

Let your mind wander to the concept of curiosity. How do you feel about your curiosity? Do you have a good relationship with your curiosity? Contemplate the role of curiosity in your life.

Give your curiosity a name, like Whiskers. Engage in a conversation with Whiskers. If you are naturally curious it should be rather easy to hear its voice and hear the name it wants to be called. If you tend to be more cautious it may take some time to hear that voice clearly. (Pause.)

Ask your curiosity to tell you how to be more connected with it. Listen to what is needed to bring your curiosity out more often. How can you have a healthy relationship with your curiosity? (Pause.)

Sit in conversation with your curiosity for as long as you want. When you feel ready, bring your focus back to your breath. Breathe in and out, paying attention to the flow of air as it comes and goes in your body.

When you are ready, open your eyes, slowly get up, and write down anything important or interesting in your journal.

Interpersonal Development

The following exercises will help your creativity grow in relation to others. Through this next section you will be able to discover how to honor the creativity in others and how to make sure that you take up the right amount of creative space. All that we do is connected to other people. How can you make these relationships more creative and fulfilling?

Discovering Creativity
✣ Love Artists ✣

Creativity should be fun—and maybe even easy. In order to honor creativity in your interpersonal relationships, go out and explore art. Go to a museum, attend the ballet, check out a local exhibit, watch a high school play, find several artists that you totally love. The only way you can find artists that you love is to go and see art. If you live in a more rural environment with less access to artistic endeavors, look up images online. Use sites like Instagram or DeviantArt to check out what people are creating.

Find art that you love and then share it with your friends, family, and other art lovers in your life. And make sure that you tell these artists that you love their work. Wait for them after a play, send them an email to their online shop, walk up at that exhibit and tell them their work touched you. You'll be glad you did and so will they!

Discovering Creativity
✣ Taking Up Space ✣

Many folks find it a challenge to be creative because they fear taking up too much space. They hide their skills and talents in order to make room for others who are better, more talented, or more highly skilled or trained. Creativity asks us to take up the right amount of space. Determining your "right size" may be a challenge. The following trance is a process of taking up space and discovering what is your right size. This can be done on your own or with a group of people. If you work with others through this process, make sure that you leave time afterwards to share how the experience was for each of you.

Find a time and place where you can be undisturbed for at least thirty minutes.

Trance: Sit comfortably with your feet flat on the floor. Give yourself the luxury of a breath. Breathe in and out, slowly and intentionally. Feel the air push your blood through your body. Feel your lungs expand with each inhale.

Sink into yourself and expand into your edges; this body that you have is fully and completely yours. What does it feel like to fully take up the space of your body? (Pause.) How is it to breathe into your feet and the top of your head at the same time? (Pause.) How is it to fully inhabit your body? (Pause.) Sit like this for some time, fully taking up your space. Many of us never take up our full space. Take up all of it now. (Long pause.)

Now expand that awareness. (Pause.) Inhabit the space that is right in front of you, right behind you, right above you, and right below you. (Pause) How is it to take up this much more space? (Long pause.)

What if you could expand yourself even further? (Pause.) Can you send your awareness into the sky above you? (Pause.) Can you move all the way into space to the moon, to the sun? (Pause.) What about below you? Can you send your awareness down into the ground below you? (Pause.) What about deeper than that, what about to the core of the earth? (Pause.)

Allow your awareness to come back into your body. (Pause.) What is your right size? How full is your awareness when you are taking up your full amount of space? (Pause.) Can you adjust yourself to fill up the right amount of space, not too much, not too little? (Pause.) How does it feel to be fully you in your best and right size? (Long pause.)

Return to noticing your breath, the regular inhalation and exhalation of your lungs. Let your awareness come back down into your body—again fully against the edges of your skin. (Pause.) Let yourself come back fully into this time and place, opening your eyes slowly when you feel ready.

Write down anything important or interesting that may have come up for you when your awareness was shifted.

COMMUNITY DEVELOPMENT

Creativity serves our communities. In many places around the world, access to museums is free. In many places, access to museums is free on certain days of the year or for locals. Finding access to artwork and the art that is being created by your local community can tell you a lot about what is going on in your corner of the world. The following exercise is designed to help you tap into that community creativity.

DISCOVERING CREATIVITY
◎❧ Art Project ☙◎

It would be impossible to dig into the energy of creativity without creating something. Perhaps you are already a skilled artist, perhaps not. It doesn't matter. What does matter is that you create something. The possibilities are endless, which may feel daunting. But choose a medium that requires you to use your hands: paint, sculpt, make a collage, draw, carve, cut, paste, or glue. Do something you've never done before.

Now comes the real challenge. Once you have completed the project, give it away. Maybe you give this as a gift to a friend or family member. Perhaps you share your creation on social media. Maybe you leave your artwork in a place for someone to stumble across and enjoy. Be brave and reveal the creativity that you possess. Imagine what creativity your bravery might inspire in others.

GLOBAL DEVELOPMENT

Creativity speaks to us in ways talking to each other never can. You can learn so much about a culture or community by their artwork and creative expressions. Imagine what the global creative message might be. The following ritual is for personal, interpersonal, and community exploration. But I encourage you to use the following ritual as a way to delve into the creative spirit of the globe.

Ritual: Mirror Scrying

This ritual is to practice divination using your beauty mirror as the divinatory mode. Divination is a tool to help you tap into your own natural intuitive psychic abilities. As with everything in life, this may be easier for some folks than it is for others. Scrying takes patience—and the right tool.

One of my mentors practiced scrying into a crystal ball for years with no success. She believed that she just wasn't gifted with that skill. Her partner suggested she try using a different type of stone than quartz crystal. So she tried a black obsidian sphere. This was an amazing success for her.

If you try scrying with your beauty mirror and don't get good results, keep practicing. If after several tries of mirror scrying you still have no results, try a different object. If your beauty mirror doesn't work, try a black mirror. Just keep practicing.

Supplies: Your beauty mirror, a candle, and your journal.
Set Up: On a table where you can sit comfortably, place the lit candle and your beauty mirror and have your journal handy.

Have the space be as dark as possible, only lit by the candle if you can.

Ritual: Take a deep breath and bring yourself into full awareness. Breathe deep into your belly, put your hand on your center, and let yourself settle into the current time and place.

Pick up your beauty mirror and while holding it in your hands, begin to run the Beauty Pentacle. Say the points of the pentacle out loud as the energy flows through your body: *beauty, devotion, creativity, desire, expression.* Ask to be shown how to access global creativity. When you feel ready, look into the mirror and watch your reflection for a few minutes.

Adjust the mirror so you can see the reflection of the flame in the surface of the mirror. Let your eyes go soft as you watch the flickering colors of the fire. Through your altered vision, take note of any shapes, letters, numbers, or images that come through the reflection. It is not uncommon to watch a little scene play out in the candle flame. If you notice your thoughts getting pulled away or distracted, just take a breath and refocus on the flame.

Write down what you see as it comes across your vision. Don't worry about the images making sense or fitting into a specific situation. Messages from scrying don't always make linear sense or have a clear and obvious point. Just write down anything you see.

When the images stop flowing or you feel complete in this process, thank your mirror for its wisdom. Thank the candle flame for its wisdom and then blow it out. Turn on some lights and read through your notes. Start to put the pieces of what came through together. Does anything obvious stand out? Are there any clear messages? Is there a message that you need to follow up on?

Final Creativity Ritual

For this ritual you will need several hours to devote to the process. This ritual is designed for a solitary practitioner but could be easily adapted for a group.

Supplies: Athame, vase of flowers, incense, bowl of salt water, a stone or crystal, your purple candle, art supplies in whatever medium you prefer, and your favorite music.

Set Up: Play your favorite music in the background as you set up your altar. You can use your beauty altar or set up an altar just for this ritual. Set up your art supplies in a way that they can be used during your ritual. Have the vase of flowers, bowl of salt water, the stone or crystal, incense, purple candle, and athame on the altar space close by.

Ritual: Light the incense and walk it around your ritual space. When you have completed this process, use the incense smoke around your body as a smoke cleanse. Pick up your athame and draw an energetic circle around your ritual space with the blade of your knife pointing outward. Start in the north and end in the north after a full rotation.

Call upon any guides, guardians, godds, or allies that you might want to join you in this working. Invite them into your circle by speaking from your heart.

Call upon your creativity. Invite your creativity into the circle as an ally and guide. Speak from your heart and make space for your creative self to fully take up your ritual space.

Pick up your art supplies and start creating. Paint or draw, carve or sing, play drums or cut out images, make jewelry or candles, do whatever style of art that you enjoy or feel called to play with. Let this process take as long as it needs to.

When you feel complete with your art piece, take it to the altar. Run the art piece through the smoke of the incense and say this: *Blessed by the spirit of air.*

Run your art piece through the candle flame and say this: *Blessed by the spirit of fire.*

Sprinkle your art piece with the salt water and say this: *Blessed by the spirit of water.*

Set your art piece on the stone or crystal and say this: *Blessed by the spirit of earth.*

Show your art piece to any godds, ancestors, or allies that you may have invited into your ritual. Explain to them what you have made and why you decided to make this piece. Ask for their blessing and speak from your heart.

Set your artwork down in a safe place or hang it up if you can.

Step back to your altar and open your circle using your athame. Slice through the energetic barrier that you created at the beginning of the ritual, releasing the circle as you move.

Welcome back.

✦ ✦ ✦ CHECK-IN ✦ ✦ ✦
HOW'S IT GOING?

Take out your journal and consider the following questions. After working through the creativity point, how have your feelings on creativity changed? Do you find yourself noticing beauty in the world around you more often? Look back over the challenges that you've faced and write what comes up for you when you see all that you have accomplished.

Chapter 8
Desire

A roaring fire is in the stone fireplace in front of you. The room is hot and filled with a thin veil of smoke. Seven priestesses sit in a semi-circle surrounding the fire and surrounding you. You are all in prayer, chanting words in a language none of you speak, but in your heart and soul you understand the meaning of these words. Sweat beads across all of your foreheads and upper lips, but the needs of your bodies are ignored as you all continue with a single-minded focus on the chant, calling in your godd.

She stands at the edge of the bonfire. There is a chill in the night air, but next to the fire it is warm and comfortable. A few feet away there are several drummers playing a hypnotic rhythm. She can feel the beat in her bones, and her pulse quickens with desire. The drums continue and her hips begin to sway in time with their beating. Unbidden, her arms stretch out and a smile overtakes her face. She has given herself over to the desire to move her body to the sound of the music. She feels free.

A door slams open and a flurry of two bodies find their way inside the room. The two are tangled together, making it hard to tell where one begins and the other ends. The door closes behind them and a raspy low giggle escapes one of the people. They move through the space together, lips touching lips, hands moving over flesh, articles of clothing dropping to the floor. They are in deep communication with each other, but neither person is saying a word. They find their way to a soft bed entangled in each other's limbs, arms and legs moving in unison.

The work of the Beauty Pentacle begins with the activation of the beauty energy center, which flows into the energy center of devotion at your right foot, which then flows to creativity in your left hand, which then flows through your heart to desire in your right hand. Desire is more than the feeling of want. Wanting is shallow; it's a knee-jerk reaction. Desire runs deep. It is a longing, a calling, a need that pulls you in a certain direction. It can't always be explained, and it doesn't always make sense.

Desire isn't just about sex—although that is a component. Desire through the lens of the Beauty Pentacle is the motivation for anything and everything you take on. It is what makes you excited, what gets you up in the morning. Desire is the spark that brings forth action. Without desire, the Beauty Pentacle would lack any action. It would be all beautiful vistas and self-exploration. The energy center of desire is what calls you into action.

Opening up to the power of desire can bring up all sorts of challenging emotions. Perhaps you relate desire to something negative, especially if you equate desire only with sex. We receive so many confusing and complex messages about sex and desire from our over-culture. But bear in mind that desire is your birthright. You deserve to encourage desire to grow in your life. You deserve to go after your desires and turn them from a goal, plan, or idea into a reality.

Awakening desire and discovering *what* you desire can expand your passions, your motivations, and what pushes you forward. Desire helps the Beauty Pentacle to awaken even further and become alive. When you step into a solid relationship with your own desire(s), that relationship will fuel your connection to the other points on the Beauty Pentacle. Desire is the energy force that keeps things moving. When your desire is strong, it will help you see the beauty, devotion, and creativity more easily.

Desire is having a full plate of passion but also saying a resounding "Yes!" to dessert. With desire there is always room for more. Listen to your desires; take note of them. What are your dreams or the fantasies that may never come to life? How do your fantasies differ from your desires? Do you know the difference between the two? By learning about your desires and how to work more in harmony with this power, your relationship with beauty will become clearer.

Figure 5: Desire Sigil

Personal Development

The following exercises are designed to open up your relationship with desire. As you work through these sections you may discover that you hold desires you were totally unaware of or, conversely, you may discover fewer desires than you thought. By working through the personal development section, you will have opportunities to open up to desire, express your desire, and come into a better relationship with desire.

✦ ✦ ✦ Check-in ✦ ✦ ✦
WHAT IS DESIRE?

Take out your journal and write on the topic of desire. This may be a charged topic. You may equate desire with sex or intimacy. You may think about desire as a goal or quest that you are constantly pursuing. Desire may be something easy for you or it could be very elusive. How does desire show up in your life? What do you desire? How do you express that desire? Do you make space in your life to experience desire? How does desire feel? Do you make space to go after the things that you desire?

Discovering Desire
Secret Desires

We all have desires that are so secret we barely even admit them to ourselves. Some of these desires are things that we will never pursue; they are fantasies or distractions. For example, I have a secret desire to pilot a plane. I imagine I would love the feeling of flying and being in control of a plane. This is a desire that I could absolutely achieve, but it's not a real goal in my life. I feel the desire, but it is a fantasy, not something I really want to pursue.

I also have a desire to be a better musician. I don't share this desire with anyone (well, I guess I have now); it is my own secret desire. However, this is a real desire. It is something that I am privately working on. I practice playing music every day in the little moments when I am alone. I want to get better at it. I enjoy it. Playing music has always been a joyful and positive experience for me. This is a secret desire that I want to manifest.

Get out your journal and make a list of your secret desires— both the real things you want to pursue and the fantasies. Compiling this list may be a process of several days. You might be able to think of several items right off the top of your head, but don't rush it. It may take time for the rest of your desires to come to you. You want to have a nice long list of things. They can be wild and risky or simple and easy. Let your desires fill a whole page.

When you have a full list of desires, go back through your list. Pull out the words that make your heart do a flip. What calls your attention or quickens your pulse? Write a second list that contains all of those ideas from your first list that make you feel excited, proud, or titillated. Are these desires that you actually want to manifest?

Read through your second list. Which of these words connect to desires that you want to take action on right now? Pick two or three desires from your second list that you feel a call to pursue. Three things you want to take from desire to reality. Make a separate page for each of these items.

On their own pages, start crafting a plan on how you are going to manifest this desire into reality. Magick can help you create what you want, but you also need a solid and clear real-world plan. Magick is only half the battle. Consider the steps moving backwards. Start from achievement of your goal. What would the step right before that be? What about the step before that? Move backwards through time to the moment of writing that desire on a sheet of paper. What is the first step needed to get you there?

What can you do today to take the first step towards your desires? Go do it now.

Discovering Desire
⟿ Wish List ⟾

Wishes are power. Wishes are spells. The over-culture we live in knows that wishes are spells. They might be the only spells that the mainstream still holds on to. People wish on their birthday candles, stars, seeing certain numbers, pennies in wells, and loose eyelashes.

One of the things I always wish on is when all of the numbers on the digital clock are the same, like at 1:11. My son says when this happens he always wishes that it will be 1:12, so he believes that he single handedly keeps the world continuing on with his wishes.

You might have a go-to wish that you always use, but digging into your wishes can be very revealing. Pull out your journal and write the words "I wish" line after line in a long column down the page. Try to get at least thirty of them on the page. Set a timer for two minutes and then start filling in what you wish for as quickly as possible.

Write down your wishes—the big, the little, and the silly. When the timer goes off stop writing. Read back over what you have written. Are there any wishes that surprise you? Any wishes that make your stomach do a flip? Any wishes that you truly want to manifest?

Pay attention to the wishes that feel like real things you want. Set the list aside for now but refer back to it often to see what has changed over time or what you might have already manifested.

DISCOVERING DESIRE
◉◜◞ Wish Jar ◟◝◉

There is a Christian saying: "Let go and let God," and in my opinion there really is something to this. Sometimes we do need to let go and give over our wishes, fears, or worries. Handing over some of the burden of a wish or worry can take the pressure off, much like the release valve on a pressure cooker. Taking the weight off is the point of having a wish jar.

A wish jar is a place for you to put your wishes, goals, desires, and yes, even your fears. It is a place to release the pressure for yourself and trust that the jar will help to get things done. Using this magickal tool lets you let go a little bit.

The first step is to get a jar. But it doesn't have to be a literal jar. You might want to use a box, a special desk drawer, or some other container. What is important is that the container you use is beautiful and feels magickal. Start to scour the thrift shops and secondhand stores to find the perfect little box or jar for this working. If all else fails, get a simple mason jar and decorate it yourself.

When you have the right container, complete the following ritual to bless the jar and prepare it to hold and manifest your wishes and eat your fears.

Supplies: Frankincense or myrrh incense, at least one large candle, a bowl of salt water, your athame, the wish jar, your beauty mirror, fresh flowers, a small lodestone, and anointing oil.

Set Up: Put together an altar space with all of the above supplies. This could be done on your beauty altar or you could create a space just for this working. Have the wish jar in the center of all the other objects. Put all of the pieces together in a way that is pleasing to you.

Ritual: Stand in front of your altar space and light the candle and
the incense. Keep the incense burning throughout the whole
ritual. Take three long, slow breaths, bringing your full awareness into the present moment.

Feel your feet planted firmly on the ground and remember your
connection to the land below you. Feel the pressure of gravity
holding you down on the planet. When you feel ready, pick up
the incense and walk around your space in a circle going deosil. Use your hand or a fan to help spread the smoke throughout
your ritual space.

Return to the altar, set down the incense, and pick up a candle. Carry this candle around the circle, moving in a deosil direction. Return the candle to the altar and pick up the salt water.
Sprinkle the water in a circle around your ritual space, moving in
a deosil direction.

Set down the bowl of salt water and pick several of the petals off of the flowers that you have on your altar. Sprinkle these
around your ritual space, moving in a deosil direction. Return to
your altar, take a deep breath, and pick up your athame.

Hold your athame over your heart and begin to run the
Beauty Pentacle energy through your body. Continue running
the pentacle until you feel full of beauty. When you are ready, extend your arm and release the Beauty Pentacle out of your blade,
and use it to create an energetic bubble around your ritual space.

Direct the Beauty Pentacle energy around you in a circle moving deosil. Then fill in the space above and below your sphere.
When you feel complete, set your athame back down on your altar.

Pick up your wish jar. Hold it in your hands and get a solid feel
for it. Connect into it. See if it has a story to tell you. Take a moment to run it through the elements that you have on your altar as

a cleansing. Run it through the incense smoke and the flame of the candle, sprinkle it with salt water, and touch it to the flowers.

Hold it in your hands while you run the Beauty Pentacle through your body. Take the anointing oil and dress your jar with it while saying this:

I imbue this container with magick
I imbue this container with power
Hold secure all my wishes
Keep them safe in your bower

Make manifest my goals
Take it out of my hands
Give me peace to move freely
I give you control of the plan

This container approves wishes
This container eats all fears
This container is one of magick
Your new job please do hear

Grant all my best wishes
Eat all my worst fears
Bring about more wholeness
Your new job please do hear

By the power of three times three
As I will it, so mote it be!

Set your wish jar in a safe place where you will keep it going forward. This might be on an altar, but it isn't necessary. It could be kept in a cupboard, on your dresser, on the edge of a book-shelf, or any place you have room for it. Once you have it in its place, put the lodestone inside of it.

Return to your altar and pick up the athame. Use the edge of the blade to cut open the circle that you created. Slice it open moving widdershins. When you are done, clap your hands three times to release the remaining energy.

Welcome back!

You may want to add a wish or fear into your jar right away. Go for it! Anytime you feel like you need help achieving a goal or releasing a fear, write it down on a slip of paper and give it to your wish jar. Anytime your jar starts to get full, burn all of the papers inside, releasing the ashes to the wind. Do this without reading them.

Discovering Desire
✆ Choosing Joy ✆

Life is hard. We are hit with challenges over and over again. This is what it is to be alive and be human—lots of learning experiences. I've said this before, and I'll likely say it again, these words are not meant to sugarcoat hardship. Terrible things are still going to happen. But through them all, we still have a choice in our reaction to them. As one of my mentors says, "Life is full of bitter disappointments, and then we laugh."

As I write this, we are coming up on the anniversary of my beloved friend's death. She died after fighting against hard, aggressive cancer for over a year. She was very sick. She had to drive hundreds of miles every week for treatments. After a few months of treatment, she was no longer able to open her mouth and had to be on a liquid-only diet. Between treatment, medication, and diet, her last year alive on this planet was a hard one.

But she never lost her joy. Never. She always found beauty in the world around her. She found beauty in her experience. She found love and connection and possibility every single day. There were still moments of fear, sadness, anger, and shock, but every day she made space for joy.

Being her friend through this process was so hard, and yet, such a blessing. Through her struggle I was reminded again and again how much beauty there is in the world. I was reminded again and again how much love is in the world. Being a witness to her experience and her way of processing, I was reminded again and again of beauty and joy.

Making space for joy comes from a deep, strong desire to live life to the fullest. This is the lesson that my friend was able to show me. Desire in its connection to beauty requires bravery. It requires a willingness to look at beauty. This isn't always the easiest choice, but it does bring more life and more beauty into life.

✦ ✦ ✦ CHECK-IN ✦ ✦ ✦

BEAUTIFUL STRANGER

Pull out your journal and complete the following sentences:

- The word "desire" makes me feel...
- Right now, I desire...
- I feel desire in my...
- Desire is...
- I express my desire by...
- Desire feels like...

If you are feeling exceptionally brave, consider posting your responses on social media and encouraging your friends to answer too. The more that we share beauty with others and engage in these conversations, the more the doors to beauty are opened and our eyes are uncovered.

Discovering Desire
〰 Dance of the Seven Veils 〰

You may have heard of the Dance of the Seven Veils. It originates from the biblical story of Salome who did a dance in order to manipulate King Herod. It is a dance of desire manifestation. The name of the dance and what happens in the dance is not described in the biblical tales, but in 1893 Oscar Wilde wrote a play that expanded on the concept.

In his one-act play, Wilde describes the scene of the Galilean King Herod lusting after his niece and stepdaughter, begging for her to dance for him and in return he will give her anything she wishes.[26] She finally agrees, asking him, "Will you indeed give me whatsoever I shall ask?" The king promises to keep his word. "Whatsoever you desire I will give it you, even to the half of my kingdom."[27] Salome says, "I am awaiting until my slave brings perfumes to me and the seven veils, and take off my sandals." Her dance wins over the king, and when she is done he asks what she desires. She responds, "The head of Jokanaan."[28] Who is John the Baptist.

The Dance of the Seven Veils became a sensual strip tease, a taking away of the layers—much like the descent of the goddess Inanna. In the Inanna tale, the goddess must remove the external trappings of power as she moves through the layers of the Underworld.

In this exercise, the Dance of the Seven Veils is not a removing of layers or a peeling away, but rather, it is a layering on of

26. Oscar Wilde, *Salome* (London: Corundum Classics, 1994), 629.

27. Wilde, *Salome*, 629.

28. Wilde, *Salome*, 685.

beauty. This is a dance of putting on what you want, adding the things to your aura and psyche that you want. This is a dance of creating the reality that you desire.

Start this process by sitting down with your journal and making a list of the things that you desire. Make a list of the traits and attributes that you want to embody. When you have at least a dozen options, pare your list down to seven desires that you want to be, step into, or put on.

After you have your seven attributes, seek out seven pieces of clothing. These could be a dress, pair of pants, soft robe, silk scarf, top hat, or any pieces of clothing that would make you feel lush and beautiful. Name each of the pieces of clothing for one of the attributes that you want to take on. If you need to, pin a piece of paper onto the clothing to remind yourself which attribute each one represents.

Set up a playlist of music that makes you want to dance. It can be music from any genre as long as it makes you want to move your body to it. Be sure the playlist is at least an hour long so you have plenty of time to be immersed in the magick of it.

Create a space where you have enough room to dance around. If you have to push the couch back or move a table into the corner, then do it. You want to be able to shake and move your body freely. If this type of space doesn't exist where you live, see if you can borrow a friend's place. Set up a full-length mirror in the space.

Start by taking a cleansing shower or bath. Do a salt scrub or make a tea out of sage, bay leaf, hyssop, and basil and add that tea water to your bath. When the bath is finished, turn on your music and stay undressed. Lay out the clothes that you have picked with the names on them all around the room.

Start the music and let it move you. Dance as your body feels called to dance. When you are ready, pick up one of the pieces of clothing. Say the name of your desire. Feel what it might be like to embody this power. Put on the garment and feel the power of this word sink into your body. Breathe it into yourself. Move your body, taking ownership of this desire.

Repeat this process. Go to the next piece of clothing; say the desire out loud. Put it on your body and feel it sink into your skin. Dance, dance, dance. Swirl around your room, shake your hips, move your arms, laugh, and take on your desires.

Continue this process until you have taken on all of the seven veils. Dance with these newly acquired powers. What does it feel like to have taken on the attributes that you so desired? Feel it, enjoy it, dance and laugh.

When you feel ready, slow your body down, come to stillness, and drink a glass of water. Take out your journal and write some notes on what happened and how you feel. Keep the layers on for as long as you want to. When you are ready to take them off, name the attribute that you have taken on, followed with the words "I am this."

Welcome back.

✦ ✦ ✦ CHECK-IN ✦ ✦ ✦
WHAT DO I DESIRE?

Take out your journal and write the words "What do I desire?" at the top of the page. Set an alarm for five minutes and write whatever comes through for you until the timer goes off. Once the time dings, read back what you have written.

As you read through your writing, circle the words that stand out to you. Circle ten to twelve of the words that feel the most potent or important. These should be words that are charged, carry strong emotions, or evoke a reaction in you.

Take all the circled words and write them on another piece of paper. Next to each of your words write the opposite word. For example, if you have written "hot" on your list, write "cold" next to it. Now go back through this list and pick out five to seven words that bring forth positive feelings around desire.

Write these five to seven words on another sheet of paper. Create an affirmation about desire that incorporates these words. Let it be a statement of your desire and what you want to call forward. Take your time with this process, fine tune it until it is an affirmation that you love. Write it on a loose piece of paper and put it in a place where you will see it every day.

DISCOVERING DESIRE
⟢ The Feel of Desire ⟣

Our bodies can reveal a lot of helpful information in relation to the Beauty Pentacle, but especially to the point of desire. Most often we feel desire in our bodies. The following exercise should be done when you have plenty of time to contemplate desire and how your body feels after moving certain feelings through it.

Center yourself in a place that is safe and comfortable. Contemplate desire. What does this word bring up in your body? How does desire feel? Where do you first feel the thrill of desire? Is it in your belly, your gut? Is it in your sex, your thoughts, or your imagination? What are the scents that call up desire in your body? Is it freshly mowed grass, baking cookies, warm leather, or rose blossoms? What scent calls your desire to awaken? What taste brings forth the feelings of desire? Is it something rich, sweet, or tangy? Can you imagine the bite of a fresh strawberry? How does that connect to your desire? What sounds awaken your desire? What about touch?

Go through all of your senses remembering, the things that call forth desire for you.

INTERPERSONAL DEVELOPMENT

The following exercises are designed to help you connect to desire in connection with other entities. A relationship with desire doesn't mean you have to focus on human relationships. Relationships with godds, Fae beings, plants, or animals can also spark your desire energy center. Desire is important to the Beauty Pentacle because it makes us aware of our relationships, and the following exercises are designed to help you do that.

Discovering Desire
◖◗ Foot Bath ◖◗

Taking time to treat another person with intimate contact can help you open up to your desire energy. This exercise is intended to help you practice your relationship with desire in a nonsexual manner. Ideally this working would be done with at least one other person after taking a walk in beauty.

The Beauty Pentacle can feel like the work of our eyes, minds, or spirits, but our feet are also an important part of the power of this tool. Our feet carry us through the days; they take us where we need to go. Our feet are easily taken for granted.

Invite a friend, relative, or partner to do this work with you. If possible, invite several people to do this working together and set up enough bowls of water so each pair of people will have a space to work. Although this working is written for pairs of people, it can be modified for you to do on your own.

Supplies: Large tub or bowl that your feet will fit in, two cups of rose petals, half a cup of Epsom salt, a towel, enough warm water to fill the bowl, and soft music.

Set Up: Fill the bowl with warm water, Epsom salt, and rose petals and set it on the floor. Play the soft music in the background and have the towel nearby.

Ritual: Let yourself breathe and come into a place of centeredness. Sit in front of the bowl of water and allow yourself to be present. Run the Beauty Pentacle through your body. Moving from point to point, faster and faster, until you feel yourself filled with the power of it. At that point, use the first two fingers of your dominant hand to draw the Beauty Pentacle over the bowl of water, imbuing it with the energy of *beauty, devotion, creativity, desire, expression.*

Place your partner's feet in the bowl of blessed water and relax. Stay present, breathe, and relax. Stay this way for as long as you feel called to. Keep your thoughts on beautiful things or following the music that is playing. If your mind starts to wander or become distracted by stressful things, just breathe and return to your present moment. Relax.

When you feel complete, dry off your partner's feet slowly and with intention. Take care of the feet that carry your friend around. Remind your partner that their feet are part of them and they should be loved. Take the bowl of water outside and pour it out as an offering to beauty. Just be aware that you don't want to pour this water anywhere there are plants you want to keep growing. Epsom salt is not good for plants.

Switch places with your partner and start the process over again.

Discovering Desire
⟨⟨ A Beloved Green Blood ⟩⟩

Connection to another living creature can awaken the beauty of desire within us. This isn't about sexual desire, but rather a desire to care for and nurture another being. This exercise connects you with a green blood (or plant ally). Ideally for this working you will procure a small potted plant that you can keep indoors. If you have a green thumb, pick a plant that you find lovely. If you don't have a green thumb, choose a plant that doesn't need a lot of pampering.

Give your plant a name and put it in a place where you will be able to easily spend time with it. Sit with the plant and breathe. Inhale the oxygen that your plant is offering to you, and in return, exhale your carbon dioxide to the green blood. Focus on the in and out, the transferred breath between you and the plant. Let yourself go into the cycle of the breathing. Allow this process to go on for as long as you feel called.

If it isn't possible for you to have a potted plant, find a plant outdoors that you can spend time with. It could be a tree near the sidewalk or a bush in a park. It will take more work to connect with your green blood but follow the process.

Find a green blood that you can develop relationship with. Repeat the process of breathing with your plant on a daily basis. Take notes of any information that comes through while sitting with your plant. Let this relationship fuel your desire.

COMMUNITY DEVELOPMENT

The desire you experience for your community is very different from personal or interpersonal desire. The following exercises are designed to help foster your relationship with desire and your community. This gives you the opportunity to share desire with other people, with your neighborhood, and with the people you come into contact with on a daily basis. Desire isn't just about the self, but about how we feel called outside of ourselves.

DISCOVERING DESIRE
◉ Walking with Death ◉

We are only guaranteed this one fleeting life. You can honor beauty by remembering that. The only thing certain is that death will come for each and every one of us. There is no escaping it. Many people live their lives in fear because of that certainty. But rather than be afraid of the inevitable, we can walk with it as an ally that helps us to see beauty.

For this exercise, remember that this planet has an end date. That may be millions of years away, but even our planet will have a death. Each person that you encounter this week was blessed to be here on this planet at the same time as you. And each of these people are headed to their own deaths.

For the next week, with every face you see, offer a silent internal blessing that the person you are looking upon will be blessed with another day of life. Send a silent blessing that they might be gifted a few more precious human experiences. Offer each person you cross a silent blessing that they might be spared from suffering or hardship.

Every person you encounter this week may not be someone you like. You may have a coworker, family member, or community member that you really dislike. How does it feel to offer them a blessing too?

Notice how you feel this week offering everyone you meet a deeper, more intense level of compassion. How does this impact your week? How does this impact how you treat and interact with people? Make sure that you take time to journal any interesting thoughts or feelings that come through during this process.

DISCOVERING DESIRE
Sumptuous Feast

This exercise is all about taking your time, opening up to sensuality, and enjoying the process. You will need plenty of prep time to create this ritual. Depending on how much you cook, you may need a few days of prep time. Plan a long meal featuring your favorite foods—or foods that you don't eat very often. You should invite some of your favorite people to come over and ask each of them to bring a dish that they feel is sumptuous. Ask each of them to come freshly bathed, cleansed, and dressed in their favorite clothing.

Look up recipes and make dishes that are rich, sumptuous, and decadent. Spend the day preparing your meal. Have delicious drinks. Set up your space with the nicest dishes that you have. Put out the tablecloth and fabric napkins. Play music in the background.

Before beginning the feast, take a cleansing shower and put on nice clothes. Before the meal say a prayer, offering a blessing to the food and all of the people whose hands helped bring it to your table. Begin your feast. Eat slowly, tasting each bite. Chew slowly, enjoying all of it. Allow yourself plenty of space to enjoy the sumptuous feast.

Let this process go on as long as you would like. And leave the dishes for the morning.

Global Development

The following ritual will connect you to desire on a global, and even universal, level. The universe we inhabit was created from a spark of desire. Each of us carries that spark of star dust inside of us. By connecting to desire on a global scale, we can reconnect to the power that inhabits everything we see.

Ritual: Walking Through Time

This is a ritual to help you connect to the first spark of our universe. Nothing ever ends; all the stuff on the planet is the stuff that has always been here. It may change form, but it does not go away. Therefore, the memories of the first moments of the universe live within us. The first spark of the universe—the big bang—is also referred to as the first orgasm. This lives within us too.

This ritual is written for a solo practitioner, but it works very well as a group activity. You will want to wear comfortable, loose-fitting clothes. Record the trance below and play it back during your ritual.

Supplies: Instrumental music with a heavy drumbeat, an eye covering or blindfold, and food and drink for afterward.

Set Up: Clear a room so you have enough space to move around as freely as possible. Have the food and drink nearby so you can easily access them when the trance is over. Start the music before you start the trance journey. Cover your eyes or soften your vision. Stand or sit, but make sure that you can move around during this process. If you feel called to dance or sway, do it. Start the music and then begin the trance.

Trance: Breathe in and feel yourself as the center of the universe. Call in all of yourself to be present in this moment. Feel how everything revolves around you. Let the edges of yourself begin to expand and let yourself move. (Pause.)

Now begin the walk backwards in time. Move through the past week, noticing any events that took place during the previous days. (Pause.)

Go back past the last months and the last year. Continue the backwards walk through your adulthood, back through your teen years, and your childhood. Travel back to when you were a baby and further back into the womb, travel back to the moment of your conception. (Pause.)

Your life did not start at this moment. We can travel further back. Move back through the lives of your parents, whether you know anything about them or not. (Pause.) Travel back through the lives of your grandparents, whether you know anything about them or not. (Pause.) Follow the flow of life past your great-grandparents and on, further and further back through time. (Pause.)

Now that you have stepped into the flow it is easier to move backwards. You travel along, seeing the flashes of revolution, invention, art, discoveries, wars. You are carried along in the blood of your ancestors, following the flow of life back farther and farther. You move beyond cities, beyond organization, beyond agriculture. Beyond. (Pause.)

You follow the flow backwards beyond civilization to when the planet was wild. Green, lush expanses of undisturbed wilderness. You travel swiftly back as the ice grows, covering the earth in its cold embrace, and then retreats again. Over and over the dance of ice and heat share the planet. Other massive scaled and feathered creatures roam the earth and then disappear; the forests grow bigger, giant mushrooms develop. The shifting tides of the planet float past you more quickly. (Pause.)

In a blink the planet loosens its pressure, and all of the molecules that keep the planet solid and moving begin to separate, breaking apart. All of those molecules move more slowly as their dance of the universe throws them out in all directions. You float along like one of those molecules. The inky black of space filled with shining and shimmering pieces of carbon, oxygen, nitrogen, and hundreds of other atoms all swirling in a dance that takes you along with it. (Pause.)

The weaving and spinning shifts from an expansive dance into a fast, pulsing inhale, culminating all of the energy into the tiniest pinpoint. This is the moment, the moment before the climax. It is the pause between the inhale and exhale. Let your body come to stillness for just a moment and feel what it is to be in this moment of pause. Feel the anticipation of desire. (Long pause.)

Time begins to move forward again. The pinpoint of light explodes, rushing forward, expanding atoms in every direction.

And you watch as the planets form, time moving much more quickly. The ice forms and defrosts. The animals roam; the planet is covered in lush forests. Civilization rises, people expand, your lineage becomes a bloodline that fires like an arrow straight back to you. (Pause.)

Your body condenses, tightening around your spirit. You can feel the beautiful gift that is your body. Notice the edges of your body, notice your breath, notice what it is to be you. Bring your body to a place of stillness. Tap your edges and hold your hands to your belly. Breathe in deeply. (Pause.)

When you feel ready, slowly remove your eye covering. Take a moment to center yourself again, reconnecting to the current time and place.

Let yourself move slowly. Eat and drink, perhaps turn the music off or leave it playing. Write down anything important or interesting in your journal.

FINAL DESIRE RITUAL

This ritual is to integrate the desire pentacle point. It is meant to be long, leaving plenty of space for you to do what you feel called to do. This is a ritual of listening to your desires and letting them be met as appropriate. Take a full day to do this ritual, folding in the pieces that you are called to, when you are called to them. The final process of the ritual should be done last, but not until it is dark.

During this ritual, follow your desires. However, don't take action on anything that would break boundaries, personal agreements, or the law. You can plan this day in advance or let it unfold following the whims of your desires during the day. Here are some suggestions:

- Sleep in
- Take a long bath
- Go to an art gallery
- Go dancing
- Dance around your house
- Clean your kitchen
- Sit somewhere cozy and read a book
- Explore an outdoor place
- Write in your journal
- Go shopping
- Drink a glass of wine
- Have a hot cup of tea
- Eat something delicious
- Take yourself out to breakfast
- Soak in a hot tub
- Get a massage
- Take the dog for a walk
- Pick flowers
- Go for a "Sunday" drive
- Go to the movies
- Paint, draw, carve, shape clay
- Have sex
- Laugh

Before the sun sets, set up your ritual space.

Supplies: Incense, set of divination cards, a few candles, glass bowl filled with water, an egg, your journal, a beautiful amulet, a small bowl of rose water, bowl of salt, cushions or pillows to sit on, food and drink.

Set Up: Set up your ritual in the smallest room you can—a closet would be perfect. The darker you can make the room the better, but use any room that you can. Light the candles and the incense. Keep the incense burning so the smoke is thick. Have the divination cards, bowl of water, egg, journal, amulet, bowl of rose water, and bowl of salt close by.

Ritual: Calm yourself, breathe deeply and slowly, allowing yourself to come to stillness. Be fully present in the moment. Create a circle around your space using a perimeter of salt. Keep the incense burning.

Roll the egg down your body from the top of your head to the bottom of your feet. This is not easy to do, and you can't drop the egg or you have to start over. You will need to roll it down your front, down each side, and down your back. Move slowly.

When complete, crack open the egg into the glass bowl of water. Look at how the egg spreads in the water. This is much like reading tea leaves. What signs, symbols, letters, or numbers do you see in the egg? How do these signs impact where you are right now in your relationship with desire? Make note of anything important in your journal.

Sit on the cushions. Take a moment to consider desire. What do you desire right now? How would you like to move forward on your desires? What would you like to ask for guidance on— right now—regarding desire? Contemplate these questions and then pull some cards. There is a Beauty Pentacle layout in the Advanced Working Section that you might consider using. Write down anything important from your reading in your journal.

Pick up the amulet and whisper your desires to it. What do you want this amulet to bring to you? How can this amulet inspire more desire in your life? Contemplate how this amulet can encourage your desire. Whisper these desires to your amulet. Sprinkle the amulet with the rose water. Put it on.

Continue to sit in contemplation until you feel complete. Write down anything important, interesting, or odd in your journal. When finished, eat and drink before breaking open your circle.

Open your circle by sweeping up the salt and moving about your evening. Ideally you should immediately go to sleep, allowing any other messages to come in your dreams.

✦ ✦ ✦ CHECK-IN ✦ ✦ ✦
HOW'S IT GOING?

Take out your journal and write your thoughts on the following questions. After working through the desire point how have your feelings on desire changed? Do you find yourself noticing beauty in the world around you more often? Look back over the challenges that you've faced and write what comes up for you when you see all that you have accomplished.

CHAPTER 9

EXPRESSION

A woman stands alone on a small stage. There is a single spot-light shining down on her. She is clearly nervous, her eyes scanning the crowd in the small make-shift theatre. All of her friends and mentors sit in the rows of seats, watching, judging. She begins to read the poem that she has written, and with each line, she removes an article of clothing. Line by line she reveals her vulnerable feelings, and line by line she removes more clothing. At the end, she stands fully naked, in all senses of the word.

A couple is in the middle of an argument. It is an argument that they have had over and over again. The problem with this argument, the reason it never gets resolved, is because one of them doesn't fully express their true feelings. They hold back, hold it in, pretend it's not hard on them. But this holding back is felt by their partner and it causes even more tension. With a breath and a brave heart, the silent one finally reveals their true fears—they express the heart of what causes this argument. All the tension leaves the room, clarity is revealed for the first time, and the couple is able to work through the argument with fresh eyes.

He sits down at the kitchen table with a pad of paper. His relationship with his mother has never been healthy, and he is tired of holding it all. Even after distancing himself from her and cutting off all ties, he still carries all the things unsaid—everything left unexpressed. His pen starts to flow across the paper, writing down all the things that need release. He curses loudly with certain memories. He cries at others. At one point he gets up, goes for a walk around the block, and then returns to the paper and pen. His mother will never read the letter, that's not the point. He needs to get it out, clear his head, and release some of the tension. When the letter is done he steps outside and burns it, scattering the ashes to the winds.

All of the energy centers of the Beauty Pentacle flow through to the point of expression. The buildup starts at the beauty point in the top of the head. This flows down to the right foot at devotion. Then it moves up and across into the left hand with creativity. The power flows across the heart and into the right hand at the center of desire. The Goddess draws another line, leading down and across to the left foot, at this energy center of expression.

This is the point where you share your own personal beauty with the world. What is it that makes you special? What is your gift and offering to share? Expression is the point where the beautiful things you have witnessed and watched are shared with others. Through this point, the power of the Beauty Pentacle becomes more than a concept; it is a living action.

Expression asks you to show the world how fierce you are. Unlike the point of creativity, where you are encouraged to make art for art's sake, the point of expression asks you to make art for the sake of others. It doesn't matter if it is "good." It doesn't matter if it is "marketable." What does matter is that you took the risk to give it away. What matters is putting your heart out there for the world to review. Yes, this is scary. It can be hard, harsh, and painful. But the most rewarding thing a human can do is share their heart with someone and have it be truly seen.

Honoring the similarities between the words "expression" and "creativity," their energy is vastly different. Expression is speaking truth; it is a showing of your brave heart. This may be related to your creative endeavors, but it might not. With the Beauty Pentacle, the point of expression is meant for the world, for those around you. Creativity is yours, you don't have to share it, but expression demands release. These two words have similar definitions on the surface, but once you start to work with them more in-depth you will begin to understand the deep differences.

The energy of the expression point also goes beyond art or creativity and into the heart of being human. How is it that you express yourself? Stepping into beauty is an act of bravery, but you have to be able to express yourself in order to be fully immersed in beauty. How easily do you say what you feel? How honest are you with your feelings—both to others and to yourself? When you express yourself, do you run roughshod all over others? Or are you on a slow and silent boil, never releasing what causes you hardship?

Opening up to the power of expression asks you to say the hard thing that needs to be said. Expression asks you to share your joy and pain. The flow of beauty energy through your body would stay forever insular if you didn't take the step to express that beauty. Open your mouth, sing your song loudly (even if you can't carry a tune), bang your drum, do that interpretative dance, tell people you love them, and cut off old toxic relationships.

The expression point is also a point of taking stock and inventory. What stays in your life? What is healthy, joyful, and beautiful? What is painful, hard, and too heavy? Is it possible to cut off some of the painful energy? Is it possible to increase the joy in your life? Express yourself in all the beautiful and challenging ways.

Figure 6: Expression Sigil

PERSONAL DEVELOPMENT

The next section of exercises is designed to connect you into the power of expression. Through this section you may be asked to say the thing that needs to be said; you may be asked to express yourself through different mediums. Not all of the ways that you need to express yourself may feel beautiful. Do it anyway. Beauty comes from the bravery required to express your needs and desires.

✦ ✦ ✦ CHECK-IN ✦ ✦ ✦
WHAT IS EXPRESSION?

Take out your journal and make time to write on the topic of expression. What feelings does this word evoke? How does expression feel different than creativity? How is it that you currently express yourself? Are you able to express yourself clearly without stepping on others? Do you struggle to express yourself? Does expression feel like a sacred act or more trouble than it's worth? Do you make space to express your needs, your wants, your desires? What does expression feel like?

DISCOVERING EXPRESSION
Kosmesis

Kosmesis is a Greek magickal process of ritual adornment. It is a type of glamoury that works to infuse magick into your day ahead based on how you dress and get prepared. Kosmesis has been written about in the ancient Greek stories, most often involving Aphrodite, Hera, and Pandora. These goddesses used the power and magick of kosmesis to seduce the men they were after.

We are going to take the patriarchal overlay off of this for a moment. Rather than thinking of kosmesis as a way to snare a man, let's look at the ritual of kosmesis as a way to snare anything your heart desires. How you express yourself in your outer appearance will help you to achieve that goal. You could also look at it as donning your battle armor or dressing for the job you want, not the job you have.

For the next week, as soon as you wake up, determine what you want to manifest that day. Focus on your goal and then go about getting ready using the magick of kosmesis to help aid you. Adorn yourself in the clothes that will make your goal possible. Put on any jewelry or makeup that may help aid in your kosmesis spell.

Leave your house knowing that you will achieve your goals today. Your spellwork is strong, and anything you want, you will get!

Discovering Expression
ᏀᏅ A Day to Yourself ᏟᎦ

How will you express yourself today? Pick one day this week that can be just for you. From the time you first wake up until you go to sleep, a day dedicated to you expressing yourself. You may want to be creative and make art. You may want to take yourself out to a natural place. You may want to go to a movie. It doesn't really matter what you do—what is important is that you choose to do it as an expression of who you are right now in this moment.

The one caveat to this challenge is that you need to spend this day on your own. Don't call a friend to go with you. Don't invite a coven mate to come along. No bringing your spouse or kids. This is a day of your own self-expression, all on your own.

Do bring your journal along with you. Take notes throughout the day as you feel called to mark down anything interesting or unusual. Clip flowers or collect business cards or posters to include in your journal as well.

Practice kosmesis before you leave too. Have a nice solid intention to help your day of expression unfold in a way that is the most beautiful.

DISCOVERING EXPRESSION
Ꮐ Beauty Affirmation ᎒

It isn't easy to stay in the flow of beauty all of the time. For some of us it requires a sustained conscious effort. A great way to help keep beauty in your daily life is with a personal beauty affirmation.

Spend some time crafting a statement—three to five sentences long—that evokes your connection to beauty and how you want to express it. This doesn't have to be poetic or perfect. It just needs to be a few easy sentences that remind you there is beauty in the world. If writing out an affirmation feels like too much, start by going through poetry to help you find an affirmation. Poetry by Hafiz or Rumi are good choices for calling forth beauty.

Write out these words and post them on your bathroom mirror. Every time you look in that mirror, read the words as a reminder of the beauty in the world. At the very least you should see this message twice when you brush your teeth, 'cause you brush your teeth twice a day, right?

DISCOVERING EXPRESSION
Breathing Through
Ꮐ the Cauldrons of Poesy ᎒

The "Cauldron of Poesy" is an ancient Irish poem that contains seeds of information on ancient Irish spirituality. It was preserved in church writings from the sixteenth century.[29] There are several modern English translations of this poem. The writings refer to three energy centers in the human body and what these energy centers control. In her book *Irish Paganism*, Irish folklorist Morgan Daimler, referencing Erynn Rowan Laurie, says, "We are told

---

29. Morgan Daimler, *Irish Paganism: Reconstructing Irish Polytheism* (Winchester: Moon Books, 2015), 32.

in the Cauldron of Poesy that each person is born with three energetic cauldrons within them. The three cauldrons are: the cauldron of incubation, the cauldron of motion, and the cauldron of wisdom." [30] There are ways to connect with the three cauldrons as a way to hold deeper awareness of yourself.

The Cauldron of Incubation resides in the pelvic bowl. I have also heard this cauldron referred to as the Cauldron of Warming. This is the seat of our passion and energy. This is where we find our sexuality and security. The second cauldron is located in our hearts and is called the Cauldron of Motion. I have also heard this cauldron referred to as the Cauldron of Vocation. This is the seat of our work in the world. This is where we hold the power of how we love and how we connect to others. The third cauldron is our skull. This cauldron is called the Cauldron of Wisdom. It is how we connect to our god-self. This is the energy center of our spiritual being.[31]

For this exercise, lie down in a place where you can comfortably move your body. For example, the floor or a bed is best because you can move around a bit. A couch would not work.

Lie down and get comfortable. Inhale, and as you do, lift your pelvis upwards. Exhale and lower your hips back down to the floor. Continue this process: inhale—lift, exhale—lower. Speed this up. Inhale and exhale more rapidly. When your hips are on the floor, imagine drinking up earth energy as if through a straw in your perineum. Each time you lift your hips, take another sip of the earth energy.

With each sip, pull up the earth energy into your pelvic bowl. Let the power of the earth awaken the Cauldron of Warming. Take note of this energy center and how it relates to the Beauty Pentacle.

---

30. Daimler, *Irish Paganism*, 32.

31. Daimler, *Irish Paganism*, 32.

Keep breathing in, keep lifting and lowering your hips, keep pulling earth energy up. Once you feel your Cauldron of Warming fill up, continue drinking the energy up into your Cauldron of Vocation. Take note of this energy center and how it relates to the Beauty Pentacle.

Let the power of the earth fill up your Cauldron of Vocation and draw it up even further to your Cauldron of Wisdom. Take note of this energy center and how it relates to the Beauty Pentacle.

When all your cauldrons are full, stop moving your hips and let this energy fuel the Beauty Pentacle. Move through the points of the pentacle: *beauty, devotion, creativity, desire, expression.* Take time to write down anything interesting or important from your experience.

✦ ✦ ✦ CHECK-IN ✦ ✦ ✦
BEAUTIFUL STRANGER

Pull out your journal and complete the following sentences:

- The word "expression" makes me feel …
- I best express myself by …
- My expression is healthy when …
- My expression is unhealthy when …
- Expression is …
- I like expression most when …

If you are feeling exceptionally brave, consider posting your responses on social media and encouraging your friends to answer too. The more that we share beauty with others and engage in these conversations, the more the doors to beauty are opened and our eyes are uncovered.

DISCOVERING EXPRESSION
༺ Letter to the Future ༻

Writing down our goals or plans can help to manifest them more quickly. When we take the time to put our thoughts down on paper, it gives them a more solid form. You can write letters to the past, to the present, to people you will never see, to your shadows, and even to yourself in the future. This working asks you to write a letter to your future self.

Get a loose sheet of paper and sit down to write yourself a letter. Ground and center yourself, taking several large, slow breaths to help you come fully into your body. Imagine yourself a year from now. You are immersed in beauty. You are awake and aware of all the awesome things around you. Your appreciation for the greater world is strong and continues to unfold on a daily basis. Let yourself feel how easy it is to be connected to beauty, how it is like a part of you.

When you feel ready, write a thank you note to this future self. Express your gratitude for the awareness that your future self holds. Write how important beauty is to your life. Encourage your future self to keep up the good work. Thank your future self for healing a part of you that was broken and disconnected from the magick of the world around you. Share why beauty is so important.

When you are finished with this letter, fold it up and hide it. Place it in a book or a journal. Tuck it in your underwear drawer or in your spice cabinet and try to forget about it. Down the road when you come across this letter, read it. Then hide it again in a different place and keep this going—hiding and finding your beauty letter over and over again.

DISCOVERING EXPRESSION
◊◊ Honey Jar ◊◊

Although container spells have been found in cultures all over the world, sweetening jars appear to have originated in the United States through African American folk magick, which includes hoodoo, conjure, or rootwork. The idea is to use a jar (the container) with a sweetener to bring sweetness to a relationship or situation. In her book *Mules and Men*, Zora Neale Hurston shares her experience learning from the root doctors of the South. She wrote, "There was one jar in the kitchen filled with honey and sugar. All the 'sweet' works were set in this jar."[32] Traditionally these are done for love, court cases, or to improve relationships with an employer or authority figure.

For the Beauty Pentacle, create a honey jar to encourage sweetness for yourself. The following recipe contains only items that are edible and won't spoil the honey. Use the honey anytime you need a reminder of the Beauty Pentacle. Add the honey to a special tea that you intend to drink for magickal purposes. Take a tablespoon of honey to remind you of the beauty in the world and in yourself.

Ideally start this working on a full moon night. It will need to sit for thirty days or a full moon cycle.

If you are vegan, allergic to honey, or can't use honey, choose another type of sweetener. Molasses, maple syrup, or even a bowl of natural sugar will work just fine. If you are allergic to any of the ingredients listed below, leave them out. There are many items available for sale that call themselves honey, but they aren't natural honey. Make sure you read ingredient labels before purchasing.

---

32. Zora Neale Hurston, *Mules and Men* (New York: Harper Perennial Modern Classics, 2008), 215.

Ingredients

1 jar real honey
¼ cup dried rose petals
½ teaspoon dried damiana
½ teaspoon dried basil
1 pinch chili powder

Stir in all of the herbs, chanting the points of the pentacle as you stir: *beauty, devotion, creativity, desire, expression.* Say this:

Each spoonful of this honey is infused with beauty.
Many drops of anthophilous devotion.
A luscious reminder of my creativity.
A taste of my own sweet desire.
Saturated with a love of personal expression.

Using a spoon, draw the Beauty Pentacle three times into the honey pot. Say this: *By the power of three times three, as I will it so mote it be.*

Set this honey pot on your beauty altar. You can burn candles on the top of the jar when you want to infuse sweetness into any other magickal working. And after thirty days, you can eat the honey as needed or desired.

Discovering Expression
⊙᎚ᴑ Sing ᴑ᎚⊙

The challenging things that need to be expressed can sometimes get stuck in our bodies. When you notice yourself struggling to express your feelings or opinions, you might consider shaking things up by vibrating your vocal cords.

Singing engages your voice, which engages your communication center. The literal vibration from your vocal cords can help you to shake up stuck energy and make more space for you to express yourself more clearly.

To help activate the point of expression, I want you to sing. It doesn't matter if you *think* you can sing—you can sing. For the next week, incorporate singing into your daily practice. There are lots of ways that you can do this. It doesn't have to look any one way, but here are some suggestions to get you started:

- Find a chant that you love and spend ten minutes every morning reciting that chant. This could be a Pagan or Witchy chant, or if you feel so inclined, check out some Eastern mantras and chant along with them. There are thousands of them on YouTube.

- Play music that you enjoy and sing along—it could be spiritual music, pop music, rock, or whatever. The type of music doesn't matter. The singing does.

- Tone. Sometimes the only noise you can get out of your mouth is a tone. Hold a note for as long as you can, take a deep breath, and keep going.

- Sing in the shower. It seems that most people are comfortable with singing in the shower.

Open up your vocal cords and let it go.

DISCOVERING EXPRESSION
◎◡ Self-Talk ◡◎

How do you express your feelings to yourself? We all have messages that play in our heads. These may come from childhood programming, messages from our parents, hardships from the past, or unresolved wounds. I refer to these messages as "old tapes." Old tapes are messages that we are holding onto because they were created from particularly painful moments in our lives and are hard to let go of. Old tapes tell us things like we are stupid, clumsy, ugly, too loud, too much, unlovable.

Most often the voices aren't our own. They are the voice of a teacher, parent, or other authority figure from our childhoods. We may know this and even be able to hear that it's not our voice, but often, the old tapes become so ingrained into our talking selves, in our egos and psyche, that we can't differentiate them from our own inner voice.

Shutting off these tapes is very difficult work. The first step is noticing them. Begin by taking note of your self-talk. How do you talk to yourself when you are alone? What do you say to yourself when you make a mistake? What are the words that you use to refer to yourself when you are triggered or hurt?

Are you kind to yourself in moments of weakness or are you cruel? Do you say soothing things to yourself when you make a mistake, or do you call yourself stupid? Begin to take note of these moments and how you respond.

When you catch yourself being unforgiving or mean, stop the tape. Press pause and offer kindness or compassion instead. You have the power to turn the tape off. We are often much crueler to ourselves than we are to other people. What if a friend, child, or lover came to you looking for soothing after doing the "stupid" thing that you did? How would you respond to their need for comfort? How would you help them to pick themselves up and move on?

If it is easy for you to offer compassion to others but not to yourself, this is a place to start making changes. Only through compassion in our self-talk can we begin to shut off these old tapes and start creating more healing and helpful messages. Imagine recording a new message of encouragement and compassion. Spend a few weeks keeping track of the messages on your old tapes. Write them down in your journal; see if you can pinpoint the moment that message got stuck in your psyche or when that message was officially recorded on your tape.

The process of collecting your taped messages may be emotionally challenging. This can bring up baggage from the past that you may not be fully, consciously aware of. Be kind and patient with yourself as these messages come forward. Remember that these messages are not your truth; you don't have to hold them. You control the message machine.

One of the messages on my tapes is: *You can only depend on yourself.* This message was repeated to me over and over again in my youth. I had to take care of myself. I couldn't rely on a relationship, friend, or anyone else to get it done. It was up to me.

I logically understand why my mom gave me this recording. Her goal was for me to not look for marriage to give me stability. She wanted me to find my own path and make sure that I had my own money and would know how to take care of myself. However, this tape morphed into me believing that I have to do it all, be it all, and take care of it all. It has led me to become an island, thinking that I can't trust anyone else to do what needs to be done.

Over the years, there have been so many moments where this message has been reinforced. And when that happens, I can hear my mom's voice in my head: *See, there you go. I told you so.* To be clear, I don't blame my mom. She was doing her best, and how the messages have recorded into my psyche is not her fault. It's just my interpretation.

I've since changed the message of this tape. When I slide into my isolation tendencies, I play my own new recording: *You are surrounded by people who support you.* Then I call one of those people. One of those people happens to be my mom.

Look at your own tapes. When you feel ready, pick one of the messages that you are ready to change. Write it down in your journal. We need to reframe this message. How can you shift the message from a negative into a positive? Cross out the old tape, maybe using red pen. Write the reframed message underneath it.

Once you have completed this part, find a place where you can sit comfortably for at least twenty minutes. Close your eyes and visualize a tape recorder. Press the play button and listen to the old tape. Allow yourself to listen closely to the true voice this message came from. Take time to notice where you feel this message in your body.

Visualize pressing the stop button on the tape, winding that message back. This time press the record button and say your new message out loud. Repeat your new message over and over again until you can feel it alive in your body. Once you feel it is alive, press the stop button, rewind the tape, and listen to your voice with your new positive message recorded on the tape.

There may be times that the old tape starts to sneak back into action. When you notice this happening, close your eyes, take a breath, and press stop on the tape. Rewind that tape and then play it again with your voice and your positive message. Remember, you control the messages; you can change the tapes.

DISCOVERING EXPRESSION
◐ Who Are You? ◑

The following exercise is inspired by the work of Joanna Macy, who has written several books on reconnecting to the world and coming into greater conversation with the needs of the planet. In one of these books—*Coming Back to Life*—she offers an exercise, believing that "persistent inquiry helps participants to free themselves from socially constructed self-definitions and attain a realization of the inherently unlimited nature of consciousness."[33]

This work is best done with another person. Choose someone you trust to go through this process with you. It doesn't have to be someone with Witchy inclinations, but that could be helpful. This work can be hard or uncomfortable, so don't give in to fear and pass it by. Pick someone and go for it.

Sit in front of each other, close enough that your knees are touching. Set a timer for five minutes. When the timer begins, have your friend ask you the following question: "What is your identity?"

Immediately answer the question with the first thing that pops into your head. Don't pause, don't think about it, just speak. As soon as you have finished speaking, your friend should then immediately repeat the question: "What is your identity?" Again, answer with the first thing that comes to you. Repeat this over and over until your timer goes off. After the timer goes off, sit in silence for about a minute. If your friend is up for it, switch roles.

Take time afterwards to process anything interesting or surprising that came up during the questioning. Make sure that you write anything important down in your journal.

INTERPERSONAL DEVELOPMENT

The next section's exercise is designed to help you release baggage around your relationships with others. You may find that

---

33. Joanna Macy and Molly Young Brown, *Coming Back to Life: Practices to Reconnect Our Lives, Our World* (Gabriola Island: New Society Publishers, 1998), 127.

you desire approval or acclaim. By working with the expression point, you will begin to shift the need for others' approval to a focus on yourself and your own needs.

DISCOVERING EXPRESSION
⟡ Release of External Validation ⟡

It is not wrong to desire the approval of others. It is not wrong to want to be noticed. In fact, it is very human to want to be noticed and appreciated. However, when all of our motivations are based on the need to be seen, we are not operating from a place of wholeness. Rather, we are looking to the external to fill up what we may fear we are lacking.

All humans have shortcomings. How utterly boring would the world be if everyone was perfect at everything? None of us are perfect, and we shouldn't be. Letting go of the need for external validation, or for looking to others to fill us up, is ongoing work. This won't shift after one exercise or ritual, but stepping into the process of healing and changing negative patterns will slowly right the ship and bring you into a better place of wholeness within yourself.

Sit down and write a list of all the ways you seek out external validation. Remember that not all of these reasons will be bad. Getting validation for what we bring to the world is important. Write them all down. Review your list and pull out those places where you are seeking external validation for unhealthy reasons. Places where you would rather release the need for validation and feel more complete and whole within yourself.

Supplies: Fire-safe container, lighter, your beauty mirror, your list of external validation-seeking behavior, and some cleansing herbs like sage, cedar, palo santo, or copal.

Set Up: Put all of the above supplies on your beauty altar.

Ritual: Set up your beauty altar, fitting in all of the supplies. Breathe, calling in all of your parts. Continue to breathe, slowly and intentionally, until you feel fully present. Visualize placing an energetic rose in the top of each corner of the room as a boundary of protection for your working.

Pick up your beauty mirror. Read your list of external validation-seeking behaviors out loud while looking at yourself in the mirror. Do this process slowly, taking note of any areas where you feel hurt, triggered, or upset by the words you are reading. Take your time with this process. Let yourself feel the feelings as they come without judgment.

When you are finished, say the following while you burn the list:

I release what no longer serves
I step into beauty and power
I release what no longer serves
I call up my own tenacity
I release what no longer serves
I acknowledge my own strength
I release what no longer serves
I am all that I need

When your list has finished burning, light the cleansing herbs and use the smoke to clear out your aura and your altar space. Visualize the smoke clearing out anything that no longer serves from your spirit body, taking it away as the smoke rises. Continue to cleanse until you feel settled.

Draw back the roses that you energetically placed in each corner of the room. Speak out loud your gratitude for the space holding you.

It is done.

Community Development

In the following exercise you will have an opportunity to use the power of expression to help your community. The problems in the world may seem daunting, but you can take small steps in your local community to make changes. The small changes will lead to major shifts and changes in the greater world.

Discovering Expression
⟳ Seed Bombs ⟲

I've made hundreds of seed bombs throughout my life. I learned this process through the Reclaiming Tradition of Witchcraft, but its origins are ancient. It is believed that seed balls were made to help propagate crops in the Nile River by the ancient Egyptians.[34] This process was "rediscovered" by Japanese perma-culturist Masanobu Fukuoka.[35]

Fukuoka spent a lifetime watching plants, both in a strict traditional farming style and in a looser and more natural permacultural one. Over time he discovered that planting in a more random style with less measured lines, rows, and structure worked

---

34. "5 Cool Facts About Seed Balls," Student Conservation Association, accessed November 14, 2019, https://www.thesca.org/connect/blog/5-cool-facts-about-seed-balls.

35. Andrew Schreiber, "Making Seed Balls: An Ancient Method of No-till Agriculture," Permaculture News, Permaculture Research Institute, June 18, 2014, https://permaculturenews.org/2014/06/18/making-seedballs-ancient-method-till-agriculture/

better for the health and vitality of the whole ecosystem. Masanobu would scatter seeds, allowing plants to take root in random places. But he was cautious to scatter seeds of plants that would support each other. Instead of rows of plants, the gardens he created were lush and natural. Seed bombs were one of the ways he would landscape difficult places to reach.[36]

The idea is to use these small seed bombs to plant local sustainable plants in areas that are uninhabited or unreceptive to traditional methods of gardening.[37] The process is simple and can be infused with your prayers to add some of your own personal beauty to the magick. Keep in mind this process may not be legal in all areas. Be sure to check legality before taking on this magickal task.

Supplies: A bucket, soil, nontoxic self-drying compostable clay, organic compost, seeds of local plants, and water.

Set Up: Have all of your supplies handy. This is best done outside, as it can get messy.

Ritual: In the bucket, mix equal amounts of compost and clay—you will need to use your hands for this process. Slowly add small amounts of water until the clay and compost mix and have a nice consistency, much like a thick paste. Add more clay, compost, and water as needed.

Pull off a small amount of clay and make a ball about the size of a quarter. Put in the seeds as you roll the ball. Set them down on a flat surface to let them dry. This will take a few hours.

---

36. "Masanobu Fukuoka," One-Straw Revolution, accessed June 17, 2019, https://onestrawrevolution.net.

37. Margot Adler, "Environmentalists Adopt New Weapon: Seed Balls," NPR, April 15, 2009, https://www.npr.org/templates/story/story.php?storyId=103129515.

206 ✦ Chapter 9

When the seed bombs are dry, you can then spread them around town. Toss them in your own yard, toss them into empty lots, fields, or abandoned areas. After the first rain, the clay will break down and the seeds will be on their way. It may take a whole season before you see the effects of your seed bombs, but keep your eyes peeled for the beauty that you helped create.

Global Development

Starting in your local community is only the first step of expression for improving the world. In the following exercise, you will shift your focus to a more global perspective, using your power and energy to help clear the planet and bring healing.

Ritual: Blessing the Place Where You Are

This is a ritual of blessing for you and for the greater world. This ritual is best done outdoors during a waxing moon. Set up the ritual before the sun sets, and then perform the ritual after dark. The ritual is written for a solitary practitioner, but it could be easily adapted for a group by splitting up the elemental roles. This ritual is both reverent and mirthful.

Supplies: Incense in a fire-safe container, candle, bowl of water, bowl of earth, bell, athame, your journal, a vase of flowers, a large quartz crystal, and a bottle of bubbles.

Set Up: Set all of the supplies up in the center of your working space. You may want to prop things on a small table or bench, but a blanket in the center of your ritual space would be fine.

Ritual: Take a moment to breathe deeply, bringing yourself into the present. Send some roots down from your body into the earth below you. Release anything that no longer serves. As you breathe in, draw up some of that clean earth energy.

When you feel complete, send some branches up into the sky above you out of the top of your head. Release what no longer serves. As you breathe in, draw down some of the sky energy. Stand in this middle place, a conduit of earth and sky. Draw your branches and roots back in.

Pick up your athame and go to the north of your space. Run the Beauty Pentacle until you feel the power of it thrumming inside of you. Let this power flow down your hand into your athame. Direct the energy to the north, creating a solid container around your ritual space. Rotate, turning in a circle until you come back to the north. All the time you are creating your circle, visualize the power of the Beauty Pentacle creating a boundary around you. Point your athame above you, watching the power create a dome above you. Point your athame below you, completing the sphere of protection.

Return to the north, draw a large pentacle in front of you, and recite: *beauty, devotion, creativity, desire, expression*. Repeat this process facing the east, south, and west. Return to the altar and set down your athame.

Pick up the bowl of earth and move to the north. Place the bowl on the ground and then kneel down, placing your head on the ground near the bowl. Pay homage to the earth, the plants, the animals; pay homage to yourself as you connect to the earth through your third eye. Raise your head and arms and say:

Earth that is my body
Soil that is my flesh
Stone that is my bone
I bless this bowl of earth
I pray for your health and mine

I offer this blessing of my love
And circle this circle nine

Walk the perimeter of the circle nine times, sprinkling the soil as you go. Return the bowl to the altar, light and pick up the incense, and face the east. Set the burning incense on the ground and then kneel over the smoke, placing your face in the smoke's path. If you have asthma or issues with breathing, modify this for your health. Pay homage to the air, the birds, the flying creatures; pay homage to yourself as you connect to the air through your throat. Raise your head and arms and say:

Air that is my breath
Wind that is my voice
Cloud that is my song
I bless this smoke of incense
I pray for your health and mine
I offer this blessing of my love
And circle this circle nine

Walk the perimeter of the circle nine times, letting the incense smoke fill the area. Return the incense to the altar and pick up the candle, light it, and face the south. Set the lit candle on the ground, and sit before it with your hand over the flame. Pay homage to the fire, the heat, the passion; pay homage to yourself as you connect to the fire through your hands. Raise your arms and say:

Fire that is my spirit
Heat that is my passion
Flame that is my dance
I bless this finger of fire
I pray for your health and mine

I offer this blessing of my love
And circle this circle nine

Walk the perimeter of the circle nine times holding up the candle, letting the light shine. Return the candle to the altar, pick up the bowl of water, and face the west. Set the bowl of water on the ground and kneel over it, touching your lips to the surface. Pay homage to the water, the emotions, the creatures that swim; pay homage to yourself as you connect to the water through your mouth. Raise your head and your arms and say:

Water that is my blood
Moisture that is my heart
Rain that is my intuition
I bless this bowl of water
I pray for your health and mine
I offer this blessing of my love
And circle this circle nine

Walk the perimeter of the circle nine times, sprinkling the water as you go. Return the bowl of water to the altar, and sit in front of the space. Sit in contemplation of your connection to the elements and how they express themselves through you. Let this contemplation start from a more serious perspective. But as your mind wanders, think on how joyful this relationship is. Think on how amazing and silly life can be.

Feel all of the blessings that you have brought into this ritual. Feel how palpable all of the prayers and blessings that you have offered are. Let this also fill you with joy. You may want to speak things out loud or share your gratitude with your voice or a song. When you feel full of that joy, pick up the bubbles and begin to blow them.

Blow the bubbles from each of the directions. Let each small miracle sphere carry the blessings of the elements out into the world. As each bubble pops somewhere outside of your sacred space, it releases those blessings and joy that you built into the circle. Let this process go on for as long as you feel called. Be joyful, be silly, laugh, and play. Send those joyous blessings into the world.

When you feel complete, return the bubbles to the altar and pick up your athame. Use your athame to break open the bottom and top of the circle you created. Then turn to the north, again releasing the circle by cutting it through with the knife. Turn widdershins, cutting open the circle as you turn, ending up back in the north.

The work is done!

After the ritual is complete, take some time to write down any thoughts or feelings that come through. Make sure that you leave nothing behind.

Final Expression Ritual

Much of this ritual is about self-reflection. You will need plenty of space to be alone and undisturbed. Ideally you will have a comfortable place to sit. This ritual is written for a solitary practitioner but could be easily modified for a group.

Supplies: Your journal, a glass of wine or juice, and a candle.

Set Up: Light the candle, set down the glass of wine, open up your journal, and go ahead.

Ritual: Breathe in, slow and deep, at least three times. Let the air awaken you. Feel the inhale of air help push your blood through your body. Feel the inhale of air awaken your brain.

Run the Beauty Pentacle through your body, starting out slowly and then speeding up. Continue running the pentacle until you can feel your body saturated with the power of it.

Sit comfortably and allow yourself to contemplate the following questions. Leave plenty of space for your thoughts to float along without trying to control them.

- How do you express yourself? Are you a talker? Are you artistic? Do you love to cook?
- How do you show your feelings to the people that you care about? Do you need to talk about things when they come up? Do you need to process quietly? Do you hold back?
- How do you express yourself to new people? Are you easy to communicate with? Are you comfortable taking the lead? How do you feel about small talk?

For some, these questions might be easy to answer while others may need time for more contemplation and thought. Give yourself plenty of time to explore and write down anything important or interesting that comes up for you.

Make a list of how you express yourself when you are feeling the following:

- Angry
- Frustrated
- Sad
- Happy
- Joyous
- Inspired
- Successful

- Confused
- Blissful

Look back over what you have written. What comes up for you looking over the words on the page? Are there areas where you aren't expressing yourself as you would like to? Are there areas that need improvement? What is one thing you can change right now in the way that you express yourself? Make a commitment to do one thing—just one—to communicate in a way that is more in alignment with your desires.

Pick up the glass of wine or juice, and using your dominant hand, draw the Beauty Pentacle over the top of the glass. Chant the points of the pentacle as you do: *beauty, devotion, creativity, desire, expression.* State your commitment out loud. Say it like you mean it. Then drink the glass of wine.

It is done.

✦ ✦ ✦ CHECK-IN ✦ ✦ ✦
HOW'S IT GOING?

Take out your journal and consider the following questions. After working through the expression pentacle point, how have your feelings on expression changed? Do you find yourself noticing beauty in the world around you more often? Look back over the challenges that you've faced and write what comes up for you when you see all that you have accomplished.

THE FINAL LINE

The power of the Beauty Pentacle comes from the first energy center, which we call "beauty." This power sits in the top of your head. As the power builds, it flows down your body into your right foot. This energy center we call "devotion." The power continues to move. The flow moves up and across, moving into the energy center in the left hand. We call this energy center "creativity." The power keeps moving from the left hand, through the heart, into the right hand. This is the energy center we call "desire." The flow continues, shifting down and across into the left foot. This is the energy center that we call "expression." But the power doesn't stop there. The power moves again. The Goddess draws one more line over us. It shifts up again, coming back up to the top of the head. The power returns to the point where it started—at the point of beauty. The circuit is complete.

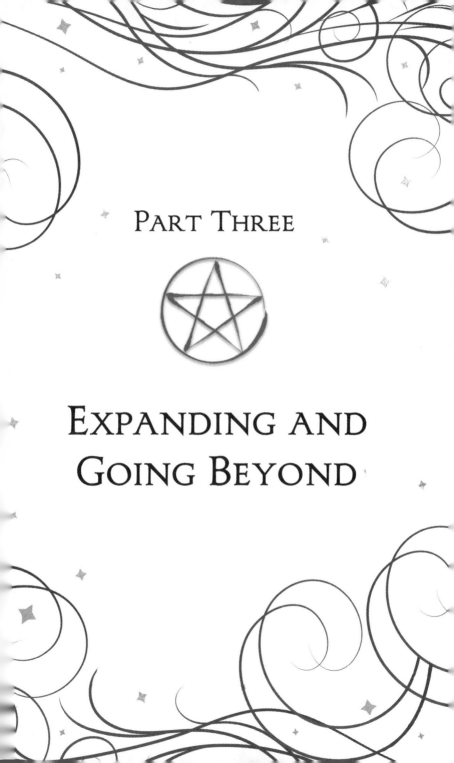

PART THREE

EXPANDING AND GOING BEYOND

Once you have worked through the points of the Beauty Pentacle, there is still more to explore. The depths of each of these points can be plumbed for months or even years. The following section will give you the opportunity to work through more advanced pentacle exercises, give you more ways to run Beauty Pentacle energy through your body, and begin looking at some of the shadows that you might need to face for the power of the Beauty Pentacle to fully incorporate.

RUNNING THE PENTACLE: ADVANCED TECHNIQUES

There are dozens of ways to run the energy of the Beauty Pentacle through your body. The more ways you run the Beauty Pentacle energy, the easier it becomes to run. By moving the energy through your body in different ways, you will discover what works best for you. The following exercises will give you a jumping-off point for moving this power through your body. Try them all and make up some of your own.

Each time you move the energy of the Beauty Pentacle through you, it gives you an opportunity to run a diagnostic. The flow of energy through the energy centers and through your body can reveal information on where you may have more work to do.

Mirror

Stand at your beauty altar with your beauty mirror close at hand. Spread your arms and legs apart and breathe, calling up the beauty of the world into the top of your head at the point of beauty. Let this energy overflow down to your right foot and the point of devotion. This power continues to move, flowing up and across into your left hand and the point of creativity. The power of beauty moves across your heart into your right hand and the point of desire. The energy flows again, across and over to your left foot and the point of expression. Finally the power flows back up to the top of your head at beauty. Allow the power to flow through you again and again, letting the energy move faster.

When you feel ready, pick up your mirror and look at the reflection of your beauty altar with the mirror. Turn the mirror and look at yourself. Run the Beauty Pentacle again, watching your own reflection as the energy flows through your body. Take note of any shifts or changes that you witness in your reflection as the Beauty Pentacle moves through your body. When you have run the pentacle at least three times, kiss your reflection and place the mirror back on the altar.

Devotionally

Practice running the energy of the Beauty Pentacle through your body as an act of devotion and a gift to the world. Go to a place where you feel connected to the spirit of devotion. This may be at your beauty altar, a shrine you've created, or another place where you might be connected into the spirit of devotion.

There is a Catholic church near my house where I spent a lot of time in prayer to the Goddess as a young woman. At the center of the church complex is a statue of Saint Elizabeth, whom I would speak to when I needed guidance. This is still a place I return to when I need to reconnect to the energy of devotion.

Once you are in your devotional space, let yourself breathe in that feeling. Fill your lungs with the power of the place and let it spread throughout your body. Let it fill you up, and then call that power up to the top of your head. Run that power through the energy centers of the Beauty Pentacle, starting at the top of your head: *beauty, devotion, creativity, desire, expression.* Let the Beauty Pentacle move through you faster and faster. When you feel full of this power, blow out a deep breath to your place of devotion as a gift.

Take a moment and feel how running the pentacle with a focus on devotion may feel differently than how you've run this energy through your body in the past. Can you feel the gift of beauty that you are moving through you and then sharing with the bigger world?

Slow and Steady

For the next week, run the pentacle as slowly as you can. Take time with the energy flow from one point to the next. Really tune in to any blockages or places where the energy moves slowly. When you hit a block, can you determine why it's there? Can you push through the blockage with your breath? Can you shift any slow spots or make more space and clarity for the beauty to flow through?

Breathe deeply and run the points of the pentacle: *beauty, devotion, creativity, desire, expression*. Take note of the color of the energy and how it moves. Let the process unfold very slowly, and make sure you write down anything you discover throughout the week.

Sensually

Using the Beauty Pentacle as a diagnostic tool can reveal where you may be experiencing imbalances in your life. Try running the Beauty Pentacle with a focus on your senses and how the power of beauty impacts them.

Call up the power of the Beauty Pentacle, and let it begin to flow through your body. Start at the top of your head at the point of beauty and let the power flow, following the points of the star: *beauty, devotion, creativity, desire, expression*. Run the Beauty Pentacle through your body three times, allowing the energy to move slowly.

As it moves from one point to the next, take note of any obstacles, sluggishness, or stuck spots. As the power of the Beauty Pentacle moves through you, take note of how this power connects to your senses. We are blessed with the senses of touch, taste, smell, sight, and hearing. How do the points of the pentacle impact your senses?

Run the pentacle again. This time hold the power at each point, starting at the point of beauty. How do your senses connect to this energy? Where do you feel beauty in your body? Explore the point of beauty in connection to your senses.

When you feel complete, let the Beauty Pentacle flow down to the point of devotion. Explore the power of this point slowly. How do your senses connect to devotion? Where do you feel devotion in your body? Explore the point of devotion in connection to your five senses.

When this feels complete, let the power of the Beauty Pentacle flow up and over to the point of creativity. Explore the power of this point slowly. How do your senses connect to creativity? Where do you feel creativity in your body and in your senses?

When this is complete, let the energy flow across to the point of desire. Explore the power of this point slowly. How do your senses connect to the power of desire? Where do you feel desire in your body and how does this connect with your senses?

When this is complete, let the energy flow down to the point of expression. Explore the power of this point slowly. How do your senses connect to the point of expression? Where in your body does expression reside and how does it connect with your senses?

Finally, let the power flow back up to the top of your head and the point of beauty. Get up slowly and carefully. Take some time to drink a glass of water. Write down any notes in your journal.

Verbalization

Our voices hold power in them. With our vocal cords, we can activate energy, clear blockages, and get things moving smoothly. With that in mind, try running the pentacle using your voice. Start at the point of beauty and say the word out loud. Keep saying the word "beauty"—over and over again—until you feel it start to thrum in your head. When you are ready, make a sound, a whoosh, a swish, a whistle, as you move the energy from beauty to devotion.

Say the word "devotion" out loud. How does it feel to say that word and feel the Beauty Pentacle? Keep saying "devotion" out loud until you feel that energy center is awake and alive. Push the energy forward to the next point. Make a noise to express that movement from devotion to creativity.

At the point of creativity, say the word out loud. Keep saying the word until you can feel the pulse of energy in the point. Let it build. Again, swoosh the energy across with a verbalization. Feel the shifting from the point of creativity to the point of desire.

Let the energy build up at the point of desire by saying the word over and over again. Let it build up and spill over. Make a sound to shift the flow of power down to the last point of expression.

Say the word "expression" over and over again, building the power up in this point. Feel it come alive. Then shift the flow of power with a sound, a swish, a noise, back up to the top of your head and the point of beauty.

Keep moving the energy through the points of the Beauty Pentacle, saying the words out loud and making noises to shift the energy from one point to the next until you feel complete. When finished, sit for another moment and let that power soak in. Take time to write down anything interesting or important that came up for you during this process.

Walking the Pentacle

A different perspective on the points of the Beauty Pentacle can be achieved by walking the pentacle. This is best done outdoors where you can draw on the ground—sidewalk chalk on pavement works great. Draw the Beauty Pentacle on the ground, leaving a space of at least three feet between the points.

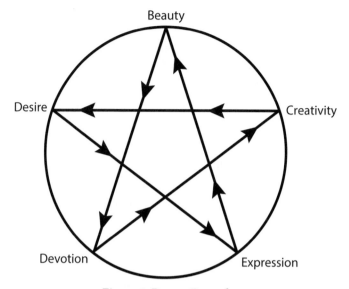

Figure 1: Beauty Pentacle

Write down the labels of the Beauty Pentacle on each of the points, following the diagram. Start by standing on the point of beauty and looking down over the pentacle. From this vantage point, you can see the points of devotion and expression in the lines below you. How is it to see the pentacle with all the connections and intersections from this vantage? Notice the flow of energy and power leading from beauty to devotion and from expression back to beauty. Take time to feel this flow of power without the other points.

When you feel ready, take the step from beauty down to the energy center of devotion. As you take these steps, notice how the flow of energy between these two points feels. How do beauty and devotion connect and feed each other?

Stand at the point of devotion and turn to face the pentacle below you. Look at how devotion is fed by the point of beauty and then feeds the point of creativity. How does this feel? When you are ready, follow the line and step onto the point of creativity, noticing as you walk how the flow of this energy between these two points moves. How do devotion and creativity feed each other?

Take the next steps to the point of creativity and face the pentacle below you. Look to the points of devotion and desire. How does it feel to have devotion feed creativity and then flow on to desire? Take note of the energy flow from creativity to desire, and step across to that point.

Face the pentacle below you while standing on the point of desire. Look at the other two points that connect to desire. How does creativity flow into desire and then flow forward into expression? Notice how the Beauty Pentacle looks and feels from this place. When you are ready, take the steps from desire to expression. How does the energy flow between these two points?

Turn and face the pentacle while standing on the energy center of expression. How does the flow of energy move from desire through expression and into beauty? Notice the flow of energy through all of the points as you stand at expression. When you feel ready, take the last steps back to the energy center of beauty, completing the pentacle. As you walk, notice how the energy flows from expression to beauty.

Step away from the pentacle and look at the shape and balance of it from a distance. How does the flow of this feel from a distance? Give yourself some time to sit in contemplation, and write down anything odd or interesting that may have come up for you during this process.

Tarot Card Layout

Use this tarot card layout when you need some insight on any blocks or obstacles that stand in the way of seeing beauty in your life. You do not need to be an expert tarot card reader to do this process. What is important is that you love the deck you are using. It could be a traditional tarot deck or an oracle deck. Just make sure that the cards appeal to you aesthetically.

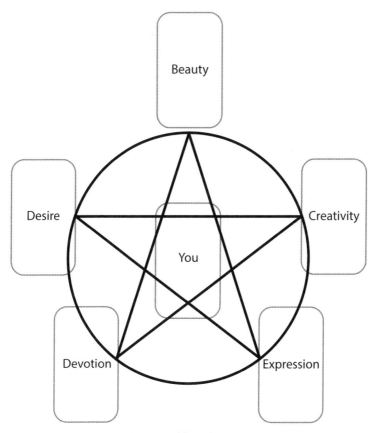

Figure 7: Tarot Layout

Take a few moments to center yourself and come to a place of stillness. Focus your mind on the question or block that you are facing. Begin to shuffle the cards, focusing on your intention for this reading. When you feel complete in your shuffling, split the deck into three piles. Pick up the piles, starting in the middle, then the right, and then the left. Fan out the cards in front of you, and using your dominant hand, draw six cards. Lay out the cards as follows:

Querent: The card in the center represents you and how you are currently connected to the question.

Beauty: The card above you is the point of beauty. This card reveals how beauty is impacting this situation and how you might shift things through the use of beauty.

Devotion: The card below your card and to the left is the point of devotion. This card can reveal your relationship to devotion, both in connection to the situation and in general.

Creativity: The card next to you on the right is the point of creativity. This card can show you where creativity can help shift the blocks or open the doors on the question.

Desire: To the left of your Q card is the point of desire. This card can show you how desire is impacting this situation. This card can show you how you might shift any blocks or bolster your current situation and what energy may be needed.

Expression: The card to the bottom right is the point of expression. This card can show you where your energy is being shown to the world. It may also indicate how to work through any obstacles through the use of expression.

After looking at all of the cards as individual points, look at how they impact each other. How do the cards connect? Where are there similar or opposing energies? Is there a flow to the cards you've chosen? How does the overall layout make you feel? There is important information in this layout that you can see by looking at each card, the patterns, and the overall flow.

Make sure to write down any readings you do in your Beauty Journal.

DIVINATION SYSTEM

Once you have a solid grasp of the Beauty Pentacle, use that energy to create your own divination system. There are lots of ways to use divination in your personal practice. Tarot cards, oracle decks, runes, bones, shells, bibliomancy, etc. There are so many types of divination that it could take more than a lifetime to learn them all. But the spirit of the Beauty Pentacle is to open to beauty and then do something with it.

In this challenge I invite you to create your own divination system. Use bits of nature, dice, coins, images, patterns, or anything that appeals to your sense of beauty. Create the symbols that call to you and then write out the meaning of the symbolism that you've created. Make it as simple or complex as you feel called to.

Once your divination system is done, practice with it. Use it to do readings for yourself. As you become more confident with doing readings for yourself, start offering readings to your friends and loved ones. Incorporate your divination system into your daily practice. Share it with the world.

MOVING THE POINTS

It might seem odd to share a magickal tool and then encourage you to change it, but that's part of the magick of the Beauty Pentacle. As I have said many times already, beauty is personal. The flow of these energies is going to feel different for you than another person. As you become more skilled and adept with running the Beauty Pentacle energy through your body, see what it might feel like to switch the points to a different order.

See if there are different words or labels that feel more in alignment with how you hold beauty. Overlay your personal words for beauty with the points of the Beauty Pentacle and then run the energy, taking note of how it feels different and how it feels the same. Let this tool be a living, evolving tool in your personal arsenal.

THE TRIANGLES OF POWER

Within the Beauty Pentacle are five triangles of power. Each of these triangles are pieces of the pie, and yet, incomplete. By working with the triangles of power, you can deepen the work of the Beauty Pentacle. If you come across obstacles or blocks in this working, diving into the triangle of power can help uncover root sources of some of the issues. Keep in mind that the triangles are concentrated, but they lack totality. The paradox of this is part of the magick.

Beauty, Devotion, Expression

Look at the diagram below. What is it to have these three points without creativity and desire? Pull out your journal and draw a triangle on the page. On each of the triangle points, write: "beauty, devotion, expression." On the next page, write the same three words across the top of a paper. Allow yourself time to free write on what comes to you when you read these words; fill the entire page.

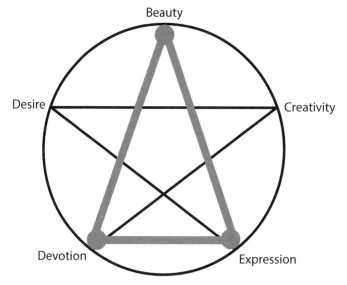

Figure 8: Triangle #1

After writing on these three pentacle points, find a place where you can lie down comfortably. Focus on the point of beauty (in your head), devotion (in your right foot), and expression (in your left foot). Let yourself feel the flow of power from each of these points, taking note of how the flow works and moves around the triangle. Write down anything important or interesting that came up during the process.

Devotion, Creativity, Beauty

Look at the diagram below. What is it to have these three points without desire and expression? Pull out your journal and draw a triangle on the page. On each of the triangle points, write: "devotion, creativity, beauty." On the next page, write the same three words across the top of the paper. Allow yourself to free write on what comes to you when you read these words; fill the entire page.

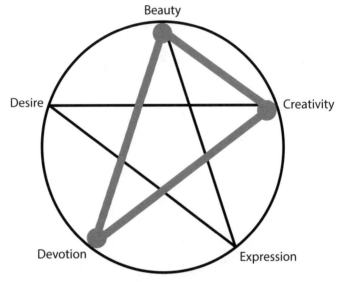

Figure 9: Triangle #2

After writing on these points, find a place where you can lie down comfortably. Focus on the points of devotion (in your right foot), creativity (in your left hand), and beauty (in your head). Let yourself feel the flow of power from each of these points, taking note of how the flow works and moves around the triangle. Write down anything important or interesting that came up during the process.

Creativity, Desire, Devotion

Look at the diagram below. What is it to have these three points without beauty and expression? Pull out your journal and draw a triangle on the page. On each of the triangle points, write: "creativity, desire, devotion." On the next page, write the same three words across the top of the paper. Allow yourself to free write on what comes to you when you read these words. Fill the page with the words that flow out.

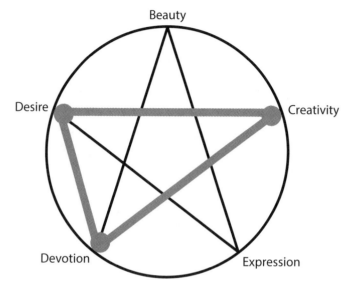

Figure 10: Triangle #3

After writing on these points, find a place where you can lie down comfortably. Focus on the points of creativity (in your left hand), desire (in your right hand), and devotion (in your right foot). Let yourself feel the flow of power from each of these points, taking note of how the flow works and moves around the triangle. Write down anything important or interesting that came up during the process.

Desire, Expression, Creativity

Look at the diagram below. What is it to have these three points without beauty and devotion? Pull out your journal and draw a triangle on the page. On each of the triangle points, write: "desire, expression, creativity." On the next page, write the same three words across the top of the paper. Allow yourself to free write on what comes to you when you read these words. Fill the page with the words that flow out.

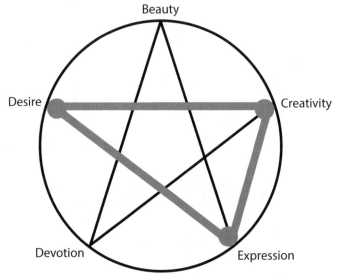

Figure 11: Triangle #4

After writing on these points, find a place where you can lie down comfortably. Focus on the points of desire (in your right hand), expression (your left foot), and creativity (your left hand). Let yourself feel the flow of power from each of these points, taking note of how the flow works and moves around the triangle. Write down anything important or interesting that came up during the process.

Expression, Beauty, Desire

Look at the diagram below. What is it to have these three points without devotion and creativity? Pull out your journal and draw a triangle on the page. On each of the triangle points, write: "ex-pression, beauty, desire." On the next page, write the same three words across the top of the paper. Allow yourself to free write on what comes to you when you read these words. Fill the page with the words that flow out.

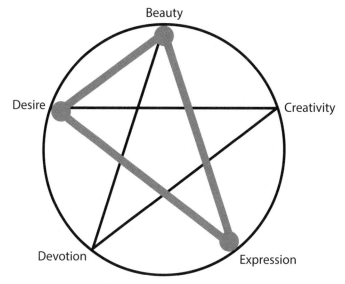

Figure 12: Triangle #5

After writing on these points, find a place where you can lie down comfortably. Focus on the points of expression (in your left foot), beauty (in your head), and desire (in your right hand). Let yourself feel the flow of power from each of these points, taking note of how the flow works and moves around the triangle. Write down anything important or interesting that came up during the process.

Overlaying the Triangles

Once you work through the triangles of power within the Beauty Pentacle, you can take the working even deeper by overlaying the triangles on top of each other. This is best done with someone else helping to guide you through the process. If that's not possible, consider recording the following exercise and playing it back for yourself.

Find a time and place where you can be undisturbed for at least thirty minutes. Ideally lie down with your arms out at your sides and your feet spread wide, making the shape of the pentacle with your body. Allow yourself to relax, taking several long, slow breaths.

Trance: When you feel ready, connect into the first triangle of power. Take note of the point of beauty at the top of your head, the point of devotion at your right foot, and the point of expression at your left foot. Allow these points to awaken, coming alive with the energy of the Beauty Pentacle. Notice how it feels to have one triangle of power moving through you. Breathe deeply.

Again, when you feel ready, overlay the second triangle right on top of the first. Take note of the point of devotion at your right foot, creativity at your left hand, and beauty at the top of your head. Let these three energy centers awaken and sink into the first set of triangles. How does it feel to have these two triangles of power running through your body? Take a moment to connect, bringing the two triangles into a place of unity. Breathe.

Now overlay the next of the triangles of power. Awaken the point of creativity at your left hand, desire at your right hand, and devotion at your right foot. Notice as these energy centers merge into the pentacle of your body and the two triangles of power already activated. How is it to now have the three merged together but the pentacle not be complete? Breathe.

When you feel ready, call forth the next triangle of power. Connect in with the point of desire at your right hand, expression at your left foot, and creativity at your left hand. Breathe into this triangle of power and connect it into the pentacle already awakened in your body. Notice the shift as another layer merges within you.

Finally, when ready, call forth the last of the triangles of power. Connect with the point of expression at your left foot, beauty at the top of your head, and desire at your right hand. Notice how this triangle of power may be different. Allow it to merge with the others. Breathe.

Allow yourself to sit with this for a few moments, the five triangles of power overlaid on each other. The pentacle points are all activated but not flowing together in linear fashion. When you feel ready, draw this energy, the power of the Beauty Pentacle, into the top of your head and begin to run the Beauty Pentacle through your body as you have so many times before. Start at beauty, moving down your right foot to devotion, up and across to your left hand and the point of creativity, across your heart and into your right hand at the point of desire, then flowing down and across your body to the point of expression, and once again coming to the top of your head and the point of beauty.

Run the Beauty Pentacle three more times, letting the power flow more quickly and easily. When you are finished, sit in silence and let the power fully sink in. Slowly open your eyes and take several deep cleansing breaths.

Allow yourself to carefully get up. Write down anything important or interesting from this experience in your journal.

Shadows and Blockages

As you run the energy of the Beauty Pentacle through your body, you may notice places where the energy is sluggish, slow, or even stuck. You may also notice dark or faded spots on the energy centers of the points. These are signs that you have work to do in connection to that energy.

Noticing these issues is the first step in clearing them. You may know right off the bat what the underlying issue is, or it may take some digging and exploration to figure out why the power is stuck. The following exercises are some ways to start clearing stuck, blocked, or diminished energy. However, if things come up that feel too big for you to process on your own, consider talking to a loved one or even seeing a therapist to help you through it. If shadows come up that feel too big, too hard, or too scary, seek outside help to best navigate those waters.

Naming the Monsters

Doing the work of the Beauty Pentacle opens up your awareness and polishes up your bright shadow. However, this can also lead to more awareness of your other shadows. The higher your bright shadow takes you, the deeper your hidden shadows will go. It's all about balance.

As you do the work of the Beauty Pentacle, take note of the hidden shadows as they start to rear their heads. Notice when your anger, jealousy, doubt, fear, or other more difficult emotions show up for you. Write it down in your journal when it happens. Write down what was going on and what happened to trigger the feelings.

In the book *Truth or Dare*, author and activist Starhawk suggests creating a monster doll to be named for your self-hater.[38] This is a way to work with your self-hater, giving it a name and a voice. We don't really want to erase our shadows—in fact, we can't. But we do need to become aware of them, integrate them, and understand their motivations.

I suggest taking this concept of the self-hater doll one step further. Name all of your monsters. Name all of the shadows that sidetrack you, try and shut you down, or try to protect you in all the wrong ways. Understand their motivations and why they say the things they say to you.

For example, one of my monsters is Perry the Procrastinator. I am a terrible procrastinator. It's because I'm a perfectionist and I fear failure. If I never start the project, I don't have to worry about failing and then I don't have to worry about it not being perfect.

However, this coping mechanism doesn't really work for me anymore. Procrastination only slows down my progress; it leaves me feeling more hurried and less in the flow with my creativity. When Perry starts telling me I should scroll through Facebook rather than work on my manuscript, I sometimes indulge him, but only with a strict time limit. Sometimes I thank him for protecting me from my perfectionism but then remind him that I really need to get to work.

Over the next few weeks, notice when your shadows show up. What is their underlying message? What are they trying to protect you from? If you could give this voice a name, what would it be? Start to keep track and engage with these parts of yourself.

---

38. Starhawk, *Truth or Dare: Encounters with Power, Authority, and Mystery* (San Francisco: Harper & Row, 1987), 144.

The more information you collect about these shadows, the more you can engage and communicate with them. What do each of them look like? How can you best communicate with them? How might you shift your relationship from one that is antagonistic to one that is complementary and helpful?

Ask Questions

When you're running the Beauty Pentacle and encounter a hole or tear in the energy sphere, notice if you already have a clear understanding of why there is a tear. If you know the answer, you can move on to working on the healing of that tear. Keep in mind that energetic healing is only half the work. You will also need to address the tear from an emotional level, which can be done with journaling, movement, exercise, writing letters, or therapy.

If you are uncertain why the hole is there, ask it questions. Focus on the weakness in the pentacle point and ask it, *What caused you, friend*? You may have to ask the question a few times before any answer comes forward. If you don't get a clear answer, leave it be and come back to it after a few days. You could also work through some of the exercises in this book connected to that specific pentacle point to shift some of the energy.

HOLES, TEARS, DARK SPOTS

While running the pentacle, if you notice spots, holes, or tears in the different energetic centers, you may have sustained wounding in that place. These are places to offer yourself healing.

Holes and Tears

A hole or tear may appear on a point of the pentacle from a trauma or difficulty that you have been unable to fully recover from. You may know right off the bat why there is damage to an energy center, or it may take some time to connect in and discover why.

Breath: When you come across a hole or a tear, the first step towards healing is to breathe into it. See if you can fill up that energy center with your breath. Breathing tends to help for smaller holes or tears. If you are dealing with a larger issue, this may not work or may only serve as a temporary solution.

Earth Energy: Next try to fill that energy center with earth energy. Lie down and inhale earth energy into your body. Start by inhaling slowly and deeply through your perineum. As you do, draw up earth energy, and then when you exhale, direct that energy into the tear or hole. Use that earth energy to fill up the empty space, as if you are creating an energetic healing patch. Repeat this process until the patch is thick and sturdy.

When you feel complete, release the earth energy and let yourself come back to center. Give yourself a couple of days and then run the Beauty Pentacle again, taking note whether the patch has held or if the hole or tear has returned. You may need to repeat this process before the patch completely heals the tear.

Sewing: For larger holes or tears, you may need to be more surgical in your healing methods. Lay down, close your eyes, and draw earth energy into your body. Visualize the earth energy turning into a needle and thread. Use that needle to sew up the tear in your energy center. Let it glow and knit together as you use the earth energy to stitch it up.

When you feel complete, release the earth energy and let yourself come back to center. This healing process may need to be redone before the healing sticks. Check back and repeat as often as possible.

Underlying Healing: As you offer healing to any weak spots, be aware that they will likely reveal what caused the damage. When you learn the root of a tear or hole in your energy field, you may re-trigger the injury, which could hold up your healing process. Healing may happen quickly, or it may take some time. If you notice healing is difficult, be kind and compassionate with yourself. It is not easy work to soothe these wounds. Engaging with therapy can help to heal holes or tears as well.

Dark Spots

A spot may appear on an energy center of the Beauty Pentacle when you have denied yourself some of the power of that point. It may appear as a dark or faded spot. These are caused when we deny our shining self or when we are trying to stay too small.

Breath: When you discover dark or faded spots on the energy centers of the Beauty Pentacle, you can breathe into them. Lie down and focus on that energy center. Use your breath as if you are blowing dust off a shelf or blowing out a candle. This may shift easily when dealing with minor spots, but for spots that have been around longer, more intensive work may be needed.

Star Fire Energy: Lie down and begin to take deep breaths, focusing on the energy of the sun. Call forward the star fire energy from the sun into your body and direct it to the dark or faded spot in the pentacle energy sphere. Focus this energy as if you were using a magnifying glass to heat up the spot. Imagine the star fire energy create a glowing heat that shines up the energy sphere and brings it back to its glow.

Shining up any faded spots in your energy centers may cause you to shine more in your regular life. People may notice a difference in you. You might speak up, stand out, or take up more space than you normally do. Let yourself shine brightly. If you fall back into old patterns, your energy centers will too.

Celebration

Upon completion of the exercises in this book, you deserve to celebrate! Make space for yourself to honor the hard work that you have done. I highly recommend giving yourself a footbath. Make it warm and luxurious. Add in rose petals and salt. Get a loofah and scrub away any rough bits. Massage sore spots. Let yourself feel spoiled for a little while.

Then adorn your feet. You may want to use a henna kit, body paints, or body markers. Draw symbols, designs, or words that inspire beauty. Decorate your feet as a reminder that every step is beautiful.

Go barefoot as much as possible so you have a visual reminder of walking in beauty. Wear sandals when you go out into the world if you can. Make it so you can see the art that you've created. Well done!

Chapter 11
Guerrilla Acts
of Beauty

The most important step of working through the Beauty Pentacle is sharing it with the world. This section is full of guerrilla acts of beauty. What is a guerrilla act? Well, the word is Spanish in origin and translates as "little war." This term was co-opted by a San Francisco mime troupe in the 1960s where they would basically do flash mobs of mime performance to protest war and other social issues of the time.

Guerrilla acts of beauty could also be considered beauty flash mobs, but done covertly—get in, get it done, get out. The goal of a guerrilla act of any sort is to replace an old broken system with a new order. With the following guerrilla acts, the goal is to bring in a new power of beauty that shifts negativity, depression, and disconnection. These activities will give you the chance to spread beauty throughout the world. The catch being that you don't get credit for it. These are covert acts done as an offering of beauty to your friends and community. Use these as a jumping-off point and then begin creating your own.

Guerrilla acts are an important part of *Walking in Beauty* because inspiring awe—giving a moment of beauty—to another person is powerful. You spread the beauty to others, and it creates an opportunity for their moment, hour, day, or life to shift. Your small—but revolutionary—guerrilla act of beauty could totally transform someone else's day. That's massive power. Best case scenario: that moment of beauty unfolds and continues. The person impacted by your guerrilla act goes on to share that experience with another person. The person then shares the story with others, and it continues like a ripple, spreading beauty to all it touches. The power of a guerrilla act of beauty goes far beyond the action that you take. That kind of power will change the world.

BEAUTY BLESSINGS

Get a stack of note paper that has a sticky back and a pen. Carry these items with you for the next week. Every time you encounter a public space with a mirror, leave a note of encouragement so the next person to visit will see it. Here are some potential beauty blessings to write:

- "You are beautiful"
- A heart shape
- "You are a blessing"
- "You are loved"
- "Thank you for your gifts"
- "Have a beautiful day"
- Your favorite affirmation

SECRET ADMIRER

We all have someone in our lives that we admire or appreciate. However, we may have never told them or don't know how to tell them. Do something nice for the person you admire today without them knowing it was from you. Here are some ideas to whet your whistle:

- Ask to speak to the manager of your favorite server. Let them know how much you appreciate their employee.

- Send flowers to a coworker.

- Write a thank you note and leave it on a friend's car window.

- Leave a plate of cookies at your neighbor's front door when they aren't home.

- Or your favorite way to show appreciation.

POP-UP SHRINES

To help spread beauty through your connection to devotion, build a shrine in secret in a public place. There are a few caveats to this process:

- It must be done in secret—no one can see you put it together.

- It must be in devotion to *something*—choose wisely.

- It must be created with all natural or biodegradable objects —don't leave litter, glitter, or plastic in an outdoor public space (or any space, really).

There is a potential problem with building a pop-up shrine. People may take your shrine down depending on where you place it. Conversely, people might begin adding to your shrine, putting their own touches and additions into what you started.

If the former happens, you have to decide whether you want to recreate your shrine or create a new one in a different spot. If the latter happens, congratulations! You've just created a working public shrine.

Clean It Up

This guerrilla act requires you to get up, get out, and do something. Go out into your favorite place and pick up litter. No matter where you live or where you like to spend your time, you will be able to find litter that needs to be dealt with. This guerrilla act can be especially powerful if you do it in a place that you are devoted to. This can become an act of beauty and an act of devotion at the same time.

Typically, a guerrilla act requires you to do things covertly and not take credit for the beauty that has been unleashed upon the world. This guerrilla act is no different, but it requires an added level of anonymity. You may spend a whole day picking up litter, and no one will notice. The work that you have done needs to be the reward, not the accolade for doing it. That is the whole point of guerrilla acts.

However, if you really want to make a difference with this guerrilla act, make it a bigger project. Organize a cleanup for your coven, family, friends, or neighborhood. Get other people involved in the process. Wait for a larger organization's cleanup date and get your people involved.

And, if spending a day physically cleaning up a space isn't something that your body can do, help organize. Make phone calls, send emails, and post on social media to help other people find out about these outdoor cleanup dates. Use your power to get as many people involved as possible.

At the very least, every time you leave your home, pick up a piece of litter and place it into a proper receptacle. Trust me, there is plenty of trash on the ground; no matter where you go, you will be able to find plenty of garbage to pick up.

Feeding the Wild

Working with beauty requires you to connect to the world around you. This includes the green bloods (or plants), animals, birds, and yes, other humans. Supporting the ecosystem around you is an important part of the Beauty Pentacle. To complete this guerrilla act, pick a wild neighbor and figure out what you can do to support the health of that being.

For example, I keep a bird feeder in my backyard all year long. This helps my local bird population during the winter. Plus, it brings me the added benefit of connecting with the winged neighbors that live in my area. It is a responsibility to keep the bird feeder clean, full, and safe from potential predators (like my cat). It is something that my family does in devotion to our little piece of land and the creatures we share it with.

Free Art Fridays

There is a social media art movement called *#FreeArtFridays*. I stumbled into this movement quite by accident. I was on a hike at a local park. About half a mile into the walk, I came across a very large canvas with a red heart painted on it. On the back of the painting was a note with the hashtag "Free Art Friday." This piece of art was left as a challenge for another artist to take the canvas and continue the painting.

I am not a painter, but I was excited about the prospect. I took the canvas home and added my own touches to the heart. It still hangs in my living room. I love it.

What I learned by following the hashtag was that every Friday local artists were leaving pieces of their artwork somewhere out in the community. Through social media and the use of the hashtag *#FreeArtFriday*, directions and hints about where the art is hiding are left like breadcrumbs for people to follow. Whoever finds the art piece first gets to keep it!

Start a Free Art Friday in your community. Use art pieces that you create, or work with friends and loved ones to create pieces just for this process of spreading beauty.

BEAUTIFUL IMAGES

Cut out beautiful images from magazines, buy a deck of beautiful tarot or oracle cards, and gather up old postcards from thrift shops and carry them with you. Any time the inspiration strikes, leave one of these images for another person to find. Here are some suggestions on where to leave your beautiful images:

- With a tip at a restaurant
- Tucked in the pages of a book at the library
- In the pocket of a coat for sale at a thrift store
- On the windshield of a car
- In the pocket of a purse or wallet for sale

SPECIAL DELIVERY

There are lots of unsung heroes in our lives. There may be people whose services you utilize on a daily basis and may take for granted. Think about the nurses, bank tellers, baristas, retail workers, delivery drivers, mail deliverers, secretaries, waitresses, and so on that work hard and often get very little appreciation back for the work that they do.

In this guerrilla act, take a moment out of your week to honor one of these people in your life. Take coffee to your favorite bank teller. Give the barista who made the coffee a bouquet of flowers. Write a note to the florist expressing your gratitude for all they do for you. Spread the beauty and pay it forward.

HELLO

For the next week, say hello to everyone you walk past. Yes, everyone. This means anyone you walk past in the hallways at work. Anyone you cross on the street. This is including anyone at the grocery store or at the dog park. Say hello to every single person. This also means saying hello to the neighbor you typically ignore or the coworker you don't really like.

This may sound too twee or easy, but a simple greeting, merely saying hello, can totally make someone else's day.

COMPLIMENTS

Spend one day over the next week in a complimentary attitude. Just for this one day, offer a sincere compliment to every single person that you encounter. The challenge here is that the compliment needs to be a sincere one. Notice how this makes you feel and notice the reactions you receive from the people you compliment.

RANDOM ACTS

Before bridge tolls in the Bay Area became automated, I would always pay the toll of the car behind me. It was a small act of kindness that cost me an extra two dollars but potentially made another person's day. There have been viral stories about someone paying for the person behind them in line at a coffee shop and this phenomenon continuing throughout the day, where each person paid for the next person in line. These simple acts don't take a lot of planning or work; that's the beauty of them. Here are a few random acts to get you started:

- Pay the bridge toll for the car behind you
- Put some coins in the meter for a street lined with parked cars
- Buy coffee for the person behind you in line at the coffee shop
- Let someone cut in front of you in line at the grocery store or movie theatre
- Leave a book in a waiting room you visit
- Hold the door open for someone
- Give up your seat on the bus

Thank You

When was the last time you wrote a thank you note? Thank you notes can be for more than wedding presents or baby shower gifts. A handwritten note used to be something that we expected; it was just good manners to send a little thank you note. But this is a lost art. We no longer take the time to send a handwritten note to thank anyone for anything.

In this guerrilla act, it's time to take up a pen and paper and write those thank you notes. If you receive exceptional service, send a thank you note. If you had a deep and moving conversation with someone, send them a thank you note. If you were given a gift, send a thank you note.

The most challenging part of this process is collecting physical addresses. Most of us don't have a lot of folks' addresses saved. But this can be part of the fun. Making handwritten notes a regular part of your practice literally mails beauty through the world.

CHAPTER 12
STAYING CONNECTED TO BEAUTY

Working through this book gives you a connection to beauty. Running the power of the Beauty Pentacle through your body helps to keep that connection strong. But life goes on. You will find yourself drawn away to the next book. You might discover a new meditation practice or spell process that you want to devote your time to. You might get hit with a bout of sadness or frustration about the state of the world and lose your connection to beauty. That's okay, and in reality, we need to understand that it is likely to happen.

It doesn't matter how many times you fall down; it matters how many times you get back up. When you notice yourself lost without beauty or stuck in a rut, there are steps you can take to get back into relationship with beauty.

DAILY PRACTICE

Daily practice is a major part of any spiritual path. What you do on a daily basis will inform the energy that you carry into the world. Crafting a solid daily practice around the Beauty Pentacle may have already evolved on its own just by doing the exercises in this book. However, if you struggle with daily practice or need more help bringing the Beauty Pentacle into your life on a daily basis, here are more suggestions for this work:

- Run the energy of the Beauty Pentacle through your body.
- Perform a guerrilla act of beauty every day.
- Take photos when you see something beautiful that you want to share.
- Intentionally adorn yourself for beauty.
- Create a playlist of songs that evoke feelings of beauty and listen to it any time you have to drive or take public transportation.
- Tell the people you love that you love them.
- Write thank you notes and letters of gratitude.
- Let yourself be awestruck as often as possible—at least on a daily basis.

Touchstones

A touchstone is a magickal object that you infuse with an energy or memory so that you may easily return to that feeling or energy when you need it the most. When you are at the height of your relationship to beauty, find a moment to be in silence. Bring yourself to stillness and begin to run the Beauty Pentacle through your body.

When you are thrumming with the power of the pentacle, pick a spot on your body to serve as a touchstone. Maybe it's your earlobe or elbow. You might also press the spot between your thumb and first finger. Press that spot and feel the energy of the Beauty Pentacle sink into that place.

Going forward, when you are feeling distant, distracted, or despondent—detached from beauty—press that place on your body and connect to the energy that you've stored there. You can make touchstones in other places too: a stone, key, or door handle. Touchstones can be set up in many places to keep you in alignment with beauty at all times.

Small Steps

One of the most important ways to stay connected to the power of the Beauty Pentacle is to surround yourself with beauty. This may mean making changes to your living space to be more in alignment with what you feel is beautiful.

You don't have to go out and spend a ton of money to shift your living environment. Make small upgrades; take baby steps towards a more beautiful space. This can be done by keeping an eye on thrift stores, estate sales, or online sales lists. By making small upgrades, you can surround yourself with beauty over time until your space is as beautiful as you would like it to be.

Conclusion

The Beauty Pentacle is something that will naturally integrate into your life because it is a natural part of living. Once you have worked through the exercises and rituals in this book, you can work through them again and again. Each time will be like peeling another layer of the onion back. Ultimately, the Beauty Pentacle is a tool. It is something that you should pull out of your toolbox when you need a reconnection to the marvel of the world around you.

Running the pentacle can be done as part of a daily practice. It can be done when you're having a rough day. It can be done when you're depressed and can't seem to find the light at the end of the tunnel. The pentacle can be run when your life is excellent and you want to celebrate. The Beauty Pentacle can be run when you are watching a sunset or the waves of the ocean crashing or looking at a spectacular view.

The Beauty Pentacle was created with the phrase *Walking in Beauty* as its action. It is a statement, a reminder, that every step is beautiful. Every time our feet touch the ground, we are connecting to beauty. We are beauty.

It is also important to remember all of the steps anyone else has taken are beautiful too. We may not always agree with others. We may not even like certain people. Our relationship with the beauty of the greater world goes beyond dogma, religion, or personal praxis. Beauty is universal. It is yours, enjoy it.

ACKNOWLEDGMENTS

The Beauty Pentacle would not exist without the lifelong programming of love and light that came from my mother. She has always been an encouraging voice and reminder of all the many blessings in life. The Beauty Pentacle has many mothers, and my mother is one of them.

This tool would also not exist if not for the encouragement and trust of Jennifer Byers, the first Witch to do this work with me. She heard my ideas and helped me to make them real. She helped me to organize my concept and gave me space to test the ideas with students. This tool would not exist in its fleshed-out form if not for the help of Irisanya Moon and Honeycomb Heart. These two Witches were on board with *Walking in Beauty* when my ancestor first charged me with the task of taking it out into the world. They both helped to add flesh to the beautiful skeleton that had already been created. I am very grateful to all of these folks, and pieces of each of them are woven into the challenges, tasks, and exercises contained in the book.

I am grateful to my spouse, Gwion Raven, and my daughter, Trinity, for being so understanding when I had a computer on my lap more nights than not. I appreciate them giving me space to pour out my ideas and use them as sounding boards when I just couldn't quite focus what I was trying to say. I am so thankful to Gwion for being my constant champion and cheerleader. I am thankful to Trinity for creating the sigils found in this book.

Thank you to the New Moon Babes who bring so much beauty, joy, and support into my life. I am so grateful to have met each and every one of you.

A giant thank you to all of the brave souls who have already started the work of the Beauty Pentacle and have been taking it out into the world for many years already. It was through the classes and workshops that this idea was solidified into a real thing.

Thank you to Seed, who taught me the joy of home adventures. Thank you to Copper, who has been a patient and kind mentor. Thank you to RoseMayDance for being an inspiration and making me believe in myself.

Big hugs and kisses of gratitude to Heather Greene for being so easy to work with, so fun to be around, and so encouraging of all the random ideas in my head. To Hanna Grimson for being on top of it and making sure everything was aboveboard. To everyone at Llewellyn; Bill, Elysia, Kat, Terry, Annie, and all the amazing people who helped bring this book to life, I am so grateful.

Gratitude, love, and unending appreciation to Ariel, Lisa, Dakota, Suzie, Polly, Elvyra, and Sequoia for being so supportive. Without all of you, the beauty that is Milk & Honey would not be possible. And truly, that place is my heart and soul.

I also must acknowledge my Taurus sun, Libra moon, and Pisces rising. Venus is strong in my chart, and I am so pleased that I have found a way to channel my desire for beauty into my work in the world. Thanks, Mom and Dad, for helping me come into the world at the exact moment I did.

Recommended Reading

Of course, the bibliography is full of books that helped to inspire and inform this book, but there are many books that are a feast of beauty. I highly recommend reading books (or listening to audio books) that have words of inspiration and make you feel beautiful and awestruck. Here is my recommended reading list of books that are fiction, nonfiction, and poetry, to bring more beauty into your life. This is just a starting point. There are so many other beautiful books in the world.

The Alchemist by Paulo Coelho
The Witch of Portobello by Paulo Coelho
Braiding Sweetgrass by Robin Wall Kimmerer
The Spell of the Sensuous by David Abram
Becoming Animal by David Abram
Milk and Honey by Rupi Kaur
Circe by Madeline Miller
GuRu by RuPaul Charles
Sastun by Rosita Arvigo

Mules and Men by Zora Neale Hurston

Ancestral Medicine by Daniel Foor

Pronoia is the Antidote for Paranoia by Rob Brezsny

The Fifth Sacred Thing by Starhawk

The Legacy of Luna by Julia Butterfly Hill

The Re-Enchantment of Everyday Life by Thomas Moore

If Women Rose Rooted by Sharon Blackie

The Rules of Magic by Alice Hoffman

Eat, Pray, Love by Elizabeth Gilbert

All About Love by bell hooks

The Prophet by Kahlil Gibran

Women Who Run With the Wolves by Clarissa Pinkola Estes

The Essential Rumi by Jalal al-Din Rumi

Pleasure Activism by adrienne maree brown

Bibliography

"5 Cool Facts About Seed Balls." Student Conservation Association. Accessed November 14, 2019. https://www.thesca.org/connect/blog/5-cool-facts-about-seed-balls.

Adler, Margot. "Environmentalists Adopt New Weapon: Seed Balls." NPR. April 15, 2009. https://www.npr.org/templates/story/story.php?storyId=103129515.

Becker, Udo. *The Continuum Encyclopedia of Symbols*. Translated by Lance W. Garmer. New York: Continuum, 2000.

Bramshaw, Vikki. *Dionysos: Exciter to Frenzy*. London: Avalonia, 2013. Kindle.

Budin, Stephanie L. *Intimate Lives of the Ancient Greeks*. Santa Barbara, CA: Praeger, 2013.

Bulfinch, Thomas. *Bulfinch's Mythology*. New York: Crown Publishers, 1979.

Cameron, Julia. *The Artist's Way: A Spiritual Path to Higher Creativity*. New York: J.P. Tarcher/Putnam, 1992.

Castellano, Deborah. *Glamour Magic: The Witchcraft Revolution to Get What You Want.* Woodbury, MN: Llewellyn Publications, 2017.

Coyle, T. Thorn. *Evolutionary Witchcraft.* New York: Jeremy P. Tarcher/Penguin, 2005.

Coyle, T. Thorn. *Make Magic of Your Life: Purpose, Passion, and the Power of Desire.* San Francisco, CA: Red Wheel/Weiser, 2013.

Crossley-Holland, Kevin. *The Norse Myths.* New York: Pantheon Books, 1980.

Cunningham, Scott. *Cunningham's Encyclopedia of Magical Herbs.* Woodbury, MN: Llewellyn Publications, 1985.

Cunningham, Scott. *The Complete Book of Incense, Oils & Brews.* Woodbury, MN: Llewellyn Publications, 1994.

Daimler, Morgan. *Irish Paganism: Reconstructing Irish Polytheism.* Winchester: Moon Books, 2015.

Dulsky, Danielle. *The Holy Wild: A Heathen Bible for the Untamed Woman.* Novato, CA: New World Library, 2018.

Faerywolf, Storm. *Betwixt & Between: Exploring the Faery Tradition of Witchcraft.* Woodbury, MN: Llewellyn Publications, 2017.

Hughes, John, dir. *Ferris Bueller's Day Off.* 1986; Los Angeles, CA: Paramount Pictures.

Hurston, Zora Neale. *Mules and Men.* New York: Harper Perennial Modern Classics, 2008.

Lafayllve, Patricia M. *Freya, Lady, Vanadis: An Introduction to the Goddess.* Denver, CO: Outskirts Press, 2006.

Macy, Joanna, and Molly Young Brown. *Coming Back to Life: Practices to Reconnect Our Lives, Our World.* Gabriola Island, BC: New Society Publishers, 1998.

Mark, Joshua J. "Nephthys." Ancient History Encyclopedia. Ancient History Encyclopedia Limited. March 13, 2016. https://www.ancient.eu/nephthys.

"Masanobu Fukuoka." *One-Straw Revolution (blog), Wordpress, accessed June 17, 2019.* https://onestrawrevolution.net/about/.

McCoy, Edain. *The Sabbats: A Witch's Approach to Living the Old Ways.* St. Paul, MN: Llewellyn Publications, 1996.

McGregor, Samuel Liddell Mathers, Aleister Crowley, and F.C. Conybeare. *The Three Magical Books of Solomon: The Greater and Lesser Keys & the Testament of Solomon.* Naples: Albatross, 2018.

Meredith, Jane, and Gede Parma. *Magic of the Iron Pentacle: Reclaiming Sex, Pride, Self, Power & Passion.* Woodbury, MN: Llewellyn Publications, 2016.

Mueller, Mickie. *The Witch's Mirror: The Craft, Lore & Magick of the Looking Glass.* Woodbury, MN: Llewellyn Publications, 2016.

Murray, Margaret A. *The Splendor That Was Egypt.* London: Biddles, 1984.

Naydler, Jeremy. *Temple of the Cosmos: The Ancient Egyptian Experience of the Sacred.* Rochester, VT: Inner Traditions, 1996.

Ruiz, don Miguel. *The Four Agreements: A Practical Guide to Personal Freedom.* San Rafael, CA: Amber-Allen Publishing, 1997.

RuPaul. *GuRu.* New York: Dey St., 2018.

Schreiber, Andrew. "Making Seed Balls: An Ancient Method of No-till Agriculture." Permaculture News. Permaculture Research Institute. June 18, 2014. https://permaculturenews. org/2014/06/18/making-seedballs-ancient-method-till-agriculture/

Spretnak, Charlene. *Lost Goddesses of Early Greece: A Collection of Pre-Hellenic Myths*. Berkley, CA: Moon Books, 1978.

Starhawk. *Truth or Dare: Encounters with Power, Authority, and Mystery*. San Francisco, CA: HarperSanFrancisco, 1987.

Sylvan, Dianne. *The Body Sacred*. Woodbury, MN: Llewellyn Publications, 2005.

Sophistes, Apollonius. "The Pythagorean Pentacle." Biblioteca Arcana. Updated January 5, 2000. http://opsopaus.com/OM/BA/PP/index.html.

Tyson, Donald. *The Fourth Book of Occult Philosophy: The Companion to Three Books of Occult Philosophy*. By Henry Cornelius Agrippa. Translated by Robert Turner. Woodbury, MN: Llewellyn Publications, 2009.

Wilde, Oscar. *Salome*. Translated by Lord Alfred Douglas. London: Corundum Classics, 1994.